Proceeds from the sale of this book are devoted to the struggle for the preservation of human liberty.

This work is dedicated to

THE CONSTITUTION

a blueprint of human organization drawn up by the wisest group of men who ever assembled for that purpose.

It is eternally true in its concept of liberty as the fundamental basis of government.

This is published in the hope of restoring the Constitution as our basic law, and preserving the liberty that it was designed to give us, against the onslaught of conspirators from without and within, so that America may become again

" . . . the land of the free . . ."

ROOSEVELT'S COMMUNIST MANIFESTO

By EMANUEL M. JOSEPHSON

Incorporating

"THE SCIENCE OF GOVERMENT FOUNDED ON NATURAL LAW"

By CLINTON ROOSEVELT

Reprint of original edition, dated 1841, of illuminist tract containing the first American publication of the plagarized Communist teachings of Adam Weishaupt, a renegade Jesuit, and the substance of the Communist Manifesto. The Roosevelt version appeared seven years before it also was plagarized by another member of the Order of Illuminati, Moses Mordecai Marx Levy, alias Heinrich Karl Marx, in Germany. It embodies a blueprint of the New Deal, its NRA and other devices, that became the tradition of the Roosevelt Dynasty. It is the pattern of an American dictatorship which they seek to impose. Their progress in imposing this dictatorship was slow until the present century. Now thanks to the support of the Rockefeller dominated "Philanthropic" Foundation Trust it is moving to ultra-rapid culmination.

TABLE OF CONTENTS

INSIGNIA OF THE ORDER OF ILLUMINATI THAT ILLUMINIST JEFFERSON MADE THE REVERSE OF U.S. SEAL

The above insignia of the Order of Illuminati was adopted by Weishaupt at the time he founded the Order, on May 1, 1776. It is that event that is memorialized by the MDCCLXXVI at the base of the pyramid, and not the date of the signing of the Declaration of Independence, as the uninformed have supposed.

The significance of the design is as follows: the pyramid represents the conspiracy for destruction of the Catholic Church, and establishment of a "One World", or UN dictatorship, the "secret" of the Order; the eye radiating in all directions, is the "all-spying eye" that symbolizes the terroristic, Gestapo-like, espionage agency that Weishaupt set up under the name of "Insinuating Brethern", to guard the "secret" of the Order and to terrorize the populace into acceptance of its rule. This "Ogpu" had its first workout in the Reign of Terror of the French Revolution, which it was instrumental in organizing. It is a source of amazement that the Catholic electorate tolerates the continuance of use of this insignia as part of the Great Seal of the U.S.

"ANNUIT COEPTIS" means "our enterprise (conspiracy) has been crowned with success". Below, "NOVUS ORDO SECLORUM" explains the nature of the enterprise; and its means "a New Social Order", or "New Deal".

It should be noted that this insignia acquired Masonic significance only after merger of that Order with Order of Illumati at the Congress of Wilhelmsbad, in 1782.

Benjamin Franklin, John Adams (Roosevelt kinsman) and Thomas Jefferson, ardent Illuminist, and defender of Adam Weishaupt, proposed the above as the reverse of the seal, on the face of which was the eagle symbol, to Congress, which adopted it on June 10, 1782. On adoption of the Constitution, Congress decreed, by Act of September 15, 1789, its retention as seal of the United States. It is stated however, by the State Department in its latest publication on the subject (2860), that **"the reverse has never been cut and used as a seal"**, and that only the obverse bearing the eagle symbol has been used as official seal and coat of arms. It first was published on the left of the reverse of the dollar bills at the beginning of the New Deal, 1933.

What is the meaning of the publication at the outset of the New Deal of this "Gestapo" symbol that had been so carefully suppressed up to that date that few Americans knew of its existence, other than as a Masonic symbol?

It can only mean that with the advent of the New Deal the Illuminist-Socialist-Communist conspirators, followers of Professor Weishaupt, regarded their efforts as beginning to be crowned with success.

In effect this seal proclaims to the peoples of the U.S. that **the entire power of their Government supports the conspiracy to undermine and destroy it and the Constitution on which it rests** — that it is **a Government of traitors.**

INTRODUCTION

Communism has been a vital factor in American politics since the very birth of our Republic. In the early days Communism was called "Illuminism." It was promoted and propagandized by a secret, conspiratorial organization that was named the Order of Illuminati, and was dedicated professedly to bringing about "a new social order", or "New Deal". Actually its purpose was to overthrow governments throughout the world by revolution and to gain for its bosses world-wide dictatorship — "One World".

This conspiracy is one of the most deeply rooted American political traditions. The members of the organization were as fanatic in their zeal as their followers, present-day Communists. This fanaticism was passed down from generation to generation, much like any other religion. As a result, the Illuminist-Socialist-Communist creed was handed down from father to son; and it became a tradition in many old American families in much the same manner as the traditional adherence of many of those families to the Masonic Order. This explains the preponderance of its adherents on the present political scene.

Clinton Roosevelt's SCIENCE OF GOVERNMENT FOUNDED ON NATURAL LAW is of high significance in American history, as the cornerstone of this traditional creed. It was plagiarized from the teachings of Adam Weishaupt, with slight modification to adapt it to the American scene, by his ranking American disciple, Roosevelt. It presents the organizational aspects of the conspiracy and is the original blueprint of the New Deal and its NRA. It is indeed astonishing that a historical document of its importance and its background history has suffered so complete a blackout as to be practically unknown to contemporaries, in whose lives it has played so large a part.

ADAM WEISHAUPT—COMMUNISM'S FATHER

Adam Weishaupt, scion of a traditionally Catholic Bavarian family that ranked high in the Church educational circle, was trained by the Jesuits. Thanks to the influence of his family in Jesuit circles, Weishaupt was made professor of Canon (or Church) law at the Ingolstadt High School, at the age of twenty four years. In the course of his training, Weishaupt had conceived a paranoid hatred of the Jesuits and of the faith of his forebears. This led him to the insanely grandiose scheme of destroying the Catholic Church and of taking over the Holy Roman Empire and the world, in a "One World" absolute dictatorship dominated by himself.

On May (1) Day, 1776, at the age of twenty-eight, Adam Weishaupt founded a secret society for the purpose of carrying out his revolutionary conspiracy, that he named the Order of Perfectibilists. Weishaupt pretended that his objective was "a new social order" and "social security" for the people, that was to be attained by "perfecting" human nature. The name of the organization he changed, shortly after its founding, to the Order of Illuminati, with the implication that its members were "enlightened", free or "liberal." The term "liberal" has since then been reserved for those who accept Weishaupt's ideas.

Weishaupt was a master propagandist and realized that "liberal" as applied to his conspiracy would become accepted because "a lie repeated often enough, comes to be believed." The extent to which this was accomplished is indicated by the fact that the day on which he founded the Order, May Day, is celebrated throughout the world by "liberals", radicals, revolutionaries, and labor organizations in recognition of the fact that it was the mother of all revolutionary organizations dedicated to class warfare in the modern era.

The task that Weishaupt had set for himself was two-fold. First was destroying the prevailing order. Second was building up a world-wide dictatorship under his domination.

The first task required the reduction of the peoples of the world to serfdom by inducing them to renounce their allegiances and wealth, or by robbing them of their possessions, and usurping power over them. To bring about renunciation of wealth, as in the rest of the conspiracy, Weishaupt unhesitatingly adopted the devices tried and proved by the very religions that he denounced and sought to destroy, as rivals for the mastery of human minds. He proclaimed that

> "Man is fallen from a condition of liberty, equality and the state of pure Nature . . . Man is not bad except as he is made so by arbitrary morality. He is bad because *religion, the State* and bad examples pervert him."

He therefore required abandonment of all the trapping of civilization, the destruction of religion, of family life and parental discipline, and of all existent governments; and he denounced ethics and morality as a violation of REASON and NATURAL LAW. The stress on NATURAL LAW as the basis of true science and human organization clearly stamps the Illuminist followers of Weishaupt, including Clinton Roosevelt.

Weishaupt alleged that existent organized religions are not true religions; that, as Clinton Roosevelt repeats, the function of true religion is:

> " . . . to feed the hungry, clothe the naked, and make on earth peace and good will to man."

This function of providing "social security" Weishaupt alleged was not served by any religion, and could be served only by his new religion, Illuminism.

However Weishaupt organized his Order along the lines of Jesuit organization and drew heavily on abandoned sections of the Canon, especially on the Canon on Usury, for his teachings. He was a ruthless politician. He was a master at the art of pretending to be all things to all men, and using men's stupidity to destroy them. He cautiously avoided shocking the religious among the initiates into the Order by pretending to support religion. He taught them that Christ was the first author of Illuminism through which he sought to lead mankind back to the original liberty and equality that had been lost after the Fall of Adam and Eve; and he exhorted his disciples to scorn riches in order to prepare the world for a community of goods that would do away with private property. But to members advanced into the secrets of the order, who were pledged to absolute discipline and "to yield to our molding hands," he taught:

> " . . the pretended religion of Christ was nothing else than the work of priests — a fraud and tyranny . . . other religions . . . have the same myths of their origin . . . are equally founded on lying, error, riddle and fraud . . . in order to destroy Christianity and all religion, we pretend to have the only true religion . . . for the end justifies the means . . . and those we have taken to deliver you and the human race from all religions, are nothing but pious frauds . . ."

But Weishaupt was a shrewd student of religion and of Canon law. He saw in the abandoned sections of the Canon law on Usury a diabolic device for robbing nations and enslaving them. This section had been abandoned because it had been found by the Church not only impractical, but actually dangerous, except possibly in Church orders where asceticism and devotion are the mainsprings and motives of existence. The rank and file of mankind engage in a struggle for existence and necessarily must be endowed with a strong sense of possession as an aid in the acquisition of material things essential for survival in the world at large. Canon law decreed that there must be "production for use and not for profit"; and that making profit in a business transaction is the sin and crime of "usury". Usury was a cardinal sin and a capital offense, under the Canon.

As a result of this Canon on Usury, the industry, commerce and civilization of the Roman Empire disintegrated and civilization and culture vanished. Only three vocations were left open to mankind: 1. Joining the orders of the Church; 2. Earning "by the sweat of the brow" as a laborer; 3. The more cunning, ruthless and violent individuals, in the role of "knight", posed as "protectors of labor", or "labor leaders", while actually enslaving the workers; and the more ruthless and violent the knight, the more serfs he enthralled, the more people he robbed, the wealthier and more powerful he became — all in the guise of "protecting" his victims and giving them "security".

The more powerful and ruthless Vandals, in no wise hampered by inhibitions imposed by the teachings of the Church, in turn vanquished the knights who were handicapped thereby; and both elements preyed on the Church itself. A man could hold his possessions or his womenfolk, and a church, monastery or convent could hold their property and wealth only so long as they were strong enough to fight for them, or able to muster others to their defense. It meant rule by labor and violence, and an end to law and order. This became the Age of Darkness that is known as Medievalism.

It reflects credit on the Church that it recognized in the Communism of Canon law on Usury the root of the evils of Medievalism; and that it abandoned that section. This prepared the way for the Renaissance, for law and order, and for the beginning of the rise of human liberty.

Professor Weishaupt knew the destructive force and the malevolent, enslaving power inherent in the Communist nature of the Canon on Usury, and he saw in it a weapon with which to impoverish and enslave mankind, and gain dominion over the world. He embraced this dross of the Church, that he planned to destroy, and made it the basis of his conspiracy. This he represented as a "new social order". He also pretended that he could root out possessivness from human nature, and thereby perfect it. This is the fundamental fallacy of Communism, even when it is sincerely tried, as has been revealed by numerous experiments during the 19th century.

For the purpose of stealthily robbing peoples of their wealth when they refused to voluntarily renounce it, Weishaupt conceived of devices for confiscating all wealth by taxation. He advocated a progressive income tax and an even more confiscatory inheritance tax that would bar transmission of wealth and concentrate it in the hands of himself as ruler. He urged the abolition of private property in any form; government ownership of industry, banking and commerce; the complete regimentation and enslavement of labor, in a discipline that required absolute submission of wealth, body and soul; and since as an educator he realized the value of education in gaining control of the minds of people (which means also control of their wealth and fortunes) and its value in gaining dominance by "brain-washing", he required government control of education. A clearer concept of his conspiracy can be had if it is borne in mind that Weishaupt's "government" in reality meant himself as dictator.

Professor Weishaupt, versed in Church lore, knew well the effectiveness of espionage, torture, terrorism, and of savagery, as devices for enforcing the subjugation and discipline of mankind. He establshed within his order for that purpose a Gestapo type terrorist and murderous espionage agency which he called "Insinuating Brothers" — to insure that there would be no leak in the secrets of the conspirators, under threat of torture and vindictive persecution, and to aid in the subjection of the citizenry. This unit got its first extensive workout in the French Reign of Terror. Every totalitarian movement that has carried on the conspiracy since then adopted this device of Weishaupt's.

The terrorist espionage corps is symbolized in the insignia of the Order of Illuminati by the "all-spying eye" mounted on a pyramid that represents the secrets of the order. It is this insignia, strangely enough, that appears on the Great Seal of the U.S.A. placed there by Weishaupt's agents in the American Colonies.

The Weishaupt-dictated Illuminist code enshrines lying, deceit, treachery, treason, brutality, violence, torture and murder, as sources of "strength" *vis a vis* the stupid diletante folks who accept civilization culture, ethics, morality and religion as their code. He taught that savagery would serve to intimidate, subjugate and terrorize their adversaries and thereby serve to speed the attainment of the conspirators' goal, which is the subjugation and enslavement of the more decent elements of mankind, and the concentration of power in their own hands.

Weishaupt taught that human life is worthless and meaningless except as a device to further his conspiracy. His followers have been instructed to lie without scruples, to deceive and betray without hesitancy. They always have been enjoined to deny their adherence to the conspiracy, to deny its Illuminist-Socialist-Communist character, when exposed; and to regularly attack and vilify their accusers, and pose as "injured parties" whose civil rights were violated. Weishaupt and his associates set the example for the conspirators by hiding their criminal activities behind aliases, a custom that still prevails among them.

The destruction of existent governments, Weishaupt planned to attain through any device that would serve to weaken and destroy them. Internally, within the nations, the recommended devices are spending the nation into bankruptcy and inflation, class warfare especially between labor and capital, revolution and civil war. The destruction wrought between nations by economic and physical warfare, however was recommended by Weishaupt as most effective in leveling down all nations to a common denominator of misery that would make them all ready prey for a dictator, and facilitate the attainment of the goal of the conspirators — One World united in serfdom under one dictator. Naturally, the attainment of this ultimate goal required the elimination of patriotism and the fostering of so-called "internationalism."

Patriotism was condemned by Weishaupt, and his followers ever since, as a vice. He wrote:

> "Nationalism, or National Love, took the place of universal love . . . Thus the origin of states or governments of civil society was the seed of discord and Patriotism found punishment in itself . . . do away with love of country and men will come once more to know and love each other . . ."

From the start, the Illuminist-Socialist-Communist conspiracy has been truly "international". From time to time its leadership has been shifted from one country to another. Agents of the conspiracy make it their careers. Weishaupt required that they worm their ways into government posts of confidence in policy-making capacities. Once a government post has been attained, the conspirators are required to promote a steady infiltration of the government by their fellow conspirators. As partners in crime, they are required to rise as a unit to the defense of their fellow conspirators; to protect them against all charges exposing their conspiratorial associations; to attack, defame and smear all persons and organizations that undertake to expose the conspiracy, and to persecute and destroy them; and to further the conspiracy in every manner and by every crime that will serve its purpose. *They are required to be traitors* to the government that employs them, and to betray those governments into the hands of the current leaders of the conspiracy, in whatever land they currently may happen to be. Conspirator agents are shifted from one land to another in key capacity, in order to insure against possible reversion to national loyalty. A prime function of "internationalism", from the viewpoint of the conspirators, is to instigate and agitate a constant chain of tension, antagonism and warfare between nations, betraying each in turn, until they are so weakened that they will fall ready prey to conspirators who bore from within.

From the point of view of the conspirators, patriotism assumes the aspects of 'isolationism", that frustrates their schemes. Treason against the rest of the world is, according to Weishaupt's "Perfectibilism", an essential and laudable trait, a "virtue" of which only his so-called "liberals" can be capable. Treason is the essential feature of what the conspirators call "internationalism". And their anthem "L'Internationale" expresses the real nature of the conspiracy.

Other essential features of the conspiracy that were dictated by Weishaupt that still characterize it today are the following:

1. A "philanthropic" pose and pretension to furthering the good of mankind, and working their "good will" on humans.
2. "Bipartisanship". Weishaupt demanded that the conspirators have no loyalty except to the conspiracy; that they never hesitate to pretend adherence to any and every cause, in the interest of

infiltrating them and taking them over for the furtherance of the conspiracy.

3. Lifetime dedication to the conspiracy. This gives it continuity during centuries. The assignment of the conspirators is perpetual, and is in many instances, hereditary, handed down from parent to offspring. During unfavorable periods for the conspiracy, its agents "go underground", continuing their activities in posts given them by fellow conspirators, that by preference are in the field of education, where they can continue their subversive propaganda among the rising generation. When the political climate becomes more favorable for the conspirators, they emerge into the open in government posts, once again carrying on. This is strikingly illustrated in the activities of Weishaupt's followers in the U. S. in recent decades. Thus adherents of Woodrow Wilson vanished from the public scene into cloistered halls, and emerged in 1933, after years of "hibernation," as the exultant agents of the New, Fair and "Ike" Deals. A consequence of the perseverance of the conspirators is the fact that, with few exceptions, most of the members of Congress, in all parties, are their agents.
4. Deceit and cunning of the conspirators who are enjoined from revealing their identification with the conspiracy and impressed with the necessity of denying their adherence. Venomous vindictiveness are visited by them on all who betray or expose them.

The extent of the "good will" towards fellow men of the Illuminists is epitomized in Weishaupt's advice to them:

> "Apply yourself to the art of counterfeiting, of masking yourself and spying on others, of picking their minds."

For the purpose of carrying out his conspiracy, Weishaupt organized his Order of Illuminati as a rigidly regimented hierarchy in which each member was pledged to secrecy (under threat of reprisal, persecution, torture and death, at the hands of the "Gestapo", symbolized by the insignia of the Order) and to absolute, unquestioning obedience and abject submission and loyalty to superiors. The members of the Order of Illuminati, like the members of their successor — the Communist Party — were intended to constitute the ruling class of a world dictatorship that would enslave all mankind. They were marshalled into several "classes" or "degrees", that in rising rank were classified roughly as follows: first, "novices", "lesser Illuminati" or "initiates"; second, "freemason — ordinary, Scottish, and Scottish knights"; and third, the "mystery classes" — including two grades of "priests", "regents", "potentates", "grand potentates", "Magus" and "King". Only the "mystery classes" were admitted to a knowledge of the criminal purposes of the Order of Illuminati.

The organization of the Order that Weishaupt conceived and created for the purpose of carrying out his brutal, destructive conspiracy that was intended to rob, despoil and enslave mankind and to restore Medievalism, that was intended to seduce mankind to overthrow its old misrulers for new ones who are even more ruthless and cruel than the old — was closely patterned on the old order which he pretended to wish to destroy. It owed much to the discipline of the Society of Jesuits, in which Weishaupt had been trained and which he hated; and to the Order of Teutonic Knights, the centuries-old group that had been granted by the Vatican the right to bring the Faith to the Slavic "heathen" at the point of the sword. They subsequently interpreted this grant as a mission to rule the world. Their motto and objective was "Deutschland uber Alles", a world dictatorship of German rulers.

Weishaupt dictated as the basic "principle" of his Order the maxim: "The end justifies the means". All concepts of civilization, of honesty, honor, decency, morality, ethics and humanity, he scorned and cast aside as the depised roots of the weakness that would betray mankind, their civilized adversaries, into the hands of the conspirators. Lying, deceit, shiftiness, dishonesty, brutality, ruthlessness and murder, he enshrined as "virtues" in the true etymologic sense of the word: "source of power". Weishaupt dictated that these "virtues" were to be inculcated into the young, rising generations through all the devices of education, entertainment and propaganda. He directed that wholesome parental discipline over them should be destroyed so as to make the children ready prey of his ghoulish crew.

From time immemorial, crafty men have connived and struggled for mastery of the *minds* of their more naive fellow men. For *control of man's mind means control of his body, his wealth, his fortune and his destiny.* Such struggle, for ostensibly benign purposes, is manifest in the history of religion. For malign purposes, it has always constituted an essential feature of every conspiracy against humanity; and is used for the creation of intolerance and hatreds that serve the purposes of the conspirators. The process of gaining control of minds *en masse,* goes by various names: education, propaganda and, in its most brutal form, "brain washing".

Professor Weishaupt, as an educator, was fully aware of how much greater is the potency of control of man's mind than control of his body. He dictated a pattern of conversion of education and all media of mass communication to subversive propaganda. This has become quite familiar to moderns through the activities of the agencies of our so-called "Philanthropic" Foundation Trust, that includes the Carnegie and Rockefeller foundations, and of all the schools, colleges and universities, newspapers, periodicals, radio, television, movies, libraries, clubs, societies and other agencies of mass communication dominated by them.

Professor Weishaupt also was the reviver of the more forceful forms of "brainwashing" made familiar to the world by the Calvary, the Inquisition, the Gestapo, the Ogpu, the NKVD, the Black Hand, in the form of his terroristic espionage organization, "Insinuating Brothers" symbolized by the pyramid-mounted eye.

Weishaupt wrote:

> "It is also necessary to gain the common people to our Order. The great means to that end is influence in the schools."

He required of his followers that they "yield themselves with perfect docility to our molding hands". It is interesting to note that the entire Occasional

Letter No. 1, issued in 1904 by John D. Rockefeller and Rev. Frederick Gates, his almoner, as a statement of the purposes of their "philanthropy", the General Education Board, is virtually paraphrased from the writings of Adam Weishaupt. Both held to the premise

> "Man is the most contemptible of all animals, because it is the only animal than can be induced to destroy itself."

Weishaupt dared go one step further than his followers. He openly expressed his contempt and openly revelled in the despicable stupidity of his brain-washed followers. Thus he wrote:

> "The most admirable thing of all is that the great Protestant and reformed theologians who belong to our Order see in it the true and genuine mind of the Christian religion. Oh! Man what can you not be led to believe?"

He demanded blind and abject adherence to the Order's "party-line" as dictated by himself, through all its deviousness, lies, contradictions, falseness and deceit — complete acceptance of mental warping and brain-washing — and unquestioning physical submission. Any follower who questioned or resisted his dictates, or who failed in abject submission, was purged. He had no scruples about saying that he sought to lure dupes into his Order; and he wrote:

> "These people swell our numbers and fill our treasury; get busy and make these folks nibble at our bait . . . but do not tell them our secrets (they are not to be admitted to the "secret degrees" and knowledge of the conspiracy to enslave them, the true purpose of the Order). They must be made to believe that the low degree that they have reached, is the highest."

It would be difficult to express more concisely the objectives of Weishaupt's conspiracy in the field of educational propaganda than was done in the above-mentioned Occasional Letter No. 1 of Rockefeller's. General Education Board. It reads as follows:

> "In our dreams, we have limitless resources and the *people yield themselves with perfect docility to our molding hands.* The present educational conventions fade from our minds,

and *unhampered by tradition, we work our own good will upon a grateful and responsive rural folk.* We shall not try to make these people or any of their children into philosophers or men of learning, or of science. We have not to raise up from among them authors, editors, poets or men of letters. We shall not search for embryo great artists, painters, musicians nor lawyers, doctors, preachers, politicians, statesmen, of whom we have an ample supply. *The task we set before ourselves is very simple as well as a very beautiful one, to train these people as we find them to a perfectly ideal life just where they are. So we will organize our children and teach them to do in a perfect way the things their fathers and mothers are doing in an imperfect way, in the homes, in the shops and on the farm."*

All the vital elements of Weishaupt's conspiracy are found in this letter. First, there is the pose of "philanthropy"; second, the intent to brain-wash, or "mold"; third, the abandonment of tradition, science and learning; fourth, the dictatorship objective; fifth, the intent to regiment the peasantry into a caste system — "just where they are"; sixth, the intent to reduce national intelligence to the lowest common denominator and to destroy parental influence (which has been so successful that it has given the country a terrifying wave of juvenile delinquency); seventh, contempt of the "peasantry" (who were also called "our children" by the tyrannic Czar, the "Little White Father"); seventh, the element of deceit (that entered the situation when the too frank avowal of the true purposes of the foundation became recognized shortly after it was founded, and the Rockefellers belied their intent to reduce intelligence to the lowest denominator, and posed as patrons of art, letters and science); eighth, the element of subversion and un-Americanism — the avowed intent to overthrow accepted customs and institutions to serve the purposes of the Rockefeller sponsors and to further their plots and schemes; and finally, "perfectibilism", the "perfecting of human nature", Weishaupt's sham.

Rockefellers, and the "Philanthropic" Foundation Trust that they have contrived, are beyond any doubt the most effective advocates, executors, and missionaries of Weishaupt's Illuminist-Socialist-Communist dictatorship program. The "brainwashing of the U.S.A., begun in 1904 through all channels of education and mass communication, over which they have usurped complete control, has been so completely effective that the American public has no suspicion or intimation of the fact that they can only think as Rockefeller wishes them to think — that they have been "trained" and "perfected" to serve Rockefeller's purpose.

Like his Rockefeller followers, and their "public relation" henchmen, Professor Weishaupt was a master propagandist. He took especial pains to lure into the Order of Illuminati the "top names" of the era among the "philosophers", authors, newsmen, and all who had at their disposal the media of mass communication; and the Order, in turn, undertook to enhance the effectiveness of the propaganda of its members by boosting and "promoting" them, in a spirit of mutual admiration. The ranks of the Order of Illuminati were filled with literati who realized the material advantages of its support. In its ranks were to be found the "Encyclopedists", Voltaire and Rousseau, who played so large a role in the preliminary propaganda that prepared the way for the French Revolution that was engineered by the Order. In Germany its ranks were joined by Goethe, Engel and Karl Marx. Marx's Communist Manifesto that publicized the administrative aspects of the Illuminist-Socialist-Communist conspiracy, was directly plagiarized from Weishaupt's teachings and writings. In America, De Witt Clinton, Thomas Paine, Thomas Jefferson and Clinton Roosevelt were among the Illuminist adherents.

Weishaupt overlooked no source of support and revenue for his "philanthropic" Order, thus setting an example that his successors have invariably followed. He undertook to be all things to all men — and women — and promised everyone fulfilment of his, or her, needs and desires, no matter how contradictory. Weishaupt organized a Ladies' Auxiliary of the Order of Illuminati that was limited to virtuous, or relatively virtuous, women, whom he promised protection of hearth and home. He also organized a Womens' Auxiliary for tramps, bums and prostitutes, to whom he promised a monopoly of the favors of the husbands of the members of the Ladies' Auxiliary. This method has been followed faithfully by Weishaupt's successors in the conspiracy.

Several groups of members offered Weishaupt special problems. The Protestant princes and rulers of Germany and Europe were delighted with Weishaupt's plan to destroy the Catholic Church, and they flocked to the Order. They brought with them control of the Masonic Order, in which they initiated Weishaupt and his fellow conspirators in 1777. Subsequently, at the Congress of Wilhelmsbad, they effected a merger of the Order of Illuminati and the Masonic Order. Weishaupt sought and welcomed the powerful support of these rulers. But he realized that he must not permit them to suspect that, in furtherance of his "internationalist" goal of One World dictatorship, the Order was dedicated to destroying them also. Weishaupt craftily solved this problem by limiting the princes and rulers to the lower degrees and barring them from the knowledge of the true purposes of the Order, that were revealed, cautiously, only to those in the higher degrees.

Renegade Jesuits, whom Weishaupt initially welcomed, then rejected, and finally welcomed once again into the Order, and Jews, who were initially rejected and later were welcomed, also constituted special problems. Eventually, however, Weishaupt and his successors welcomed into the Order these groups, and all others that could be trusted to be thoroughly discontent with the prevailing order. And it was primarily, renegade Catholics, chronic malcontents and revolutionaries among the Protestants, and Jews who were selectively advanced to the highest degrees and innermost secrets of the Order of Illuminati and its successor organizations.

In time, crafty, cunning use was made of the Jews by the Illuminist conspirators. Special Illuminist lodges were set up among them such as the Egyptian Rite of Memphis, established by Cagliostro, the Rite of Mizraim, established in Paris, and the Haskalah

(Hebrew for enlightenment, or Illuminism) in the Slavic countries. The Illuminists gained the support of the Jews by pretending to foster the movement for their liberation and release from the Ghetto. More than a century elapsed before it might have become obvious to the Jewish supporters of the Illuminist-Socialist-Communist conspiracy that their supposed liberators merely planned to impose on them, and on fellow minority dupes, far more brutal, murderous forms of serfdom and inhumanity that bear the names of National Socialism and Communism. But unfortunately most of them fail to recognize how they have betrayed themselves and have been duped into the role of catspaws who further their own destruction by becoming pawns of the master conspirators. They continue to play a prominent but minor role in the conspiracy. As a result of it, they have leaped quite literally from the frying pan into the fire — from the Ghetto to the concentration camp and its gas chamber and incinerator.

In the conspirators' plan for effecting a dictatorship, the device, of wiping out individuality through regimentation into organizations dominated by themselves in which the "faceless" rank and file are denied any voice, has been relied upon heavily. The key organizations in this regimentation have been labor unions. From the very beginning, the control of labor has been one of the first goals dictated by Adam Weishaupt. For control of labor implies control of the bulk of the populace, and control of virtually all production and services. In addition, through labor unions set up and controlled by them, the conspirators have assured themselves control of the earnings and wealth of the workers, and enabled them to levy a special tax for the privilege of working, for their own private enrichment and for the further financing of the conspiracy. It has also given the conspirators a weapon with which to blackmail on an unlimited scale (under the pretense of welfare, health funds and pensions and an endless array of devices) both industry and the community. Like the knights of Medieval times, the conspirator "labor leaders" represent that they are "protecting" labor while exploiting, despoiling, looting and blackmailing the workers. The conspirators carefully hide from their victims that the regimentation in unions is the initial stage of the conspiracy and establishes the framework of the organization that spells their actual enslavement when the ultimate goal of dictatorship is attained. Not even the most rabidly radical of the conspirators among the labor "leaders" dares deny that the workers of Soviet Russia are reduced to slavery through unionization — exactly as planned by Adam Weishaupt, and his followers, Roosevelt and Marx.

Weishaupt was a master criminal of the type that appears at rare intervals in world history, who alone can aspire to attaining mastery over the world by their utter ruthlessness, and rule it as One World, their own world. He operated as a prince of confidence men. He undertook to convince all elements of society that they would reap vast benefits — all that they desired — from his conspiracy, which was cynically designed to betray them all: workers who were to be enslaved, employers who were to be looted and ruined, rulers who were to be overthrown and executed, clergymen whose religions were to be wiped out. By the cell type of organization of the conspiracy, Weishaupt undertook to prevent the segregated groups from learning that all of them were to be betrayed, instead of being led to salvation. The conspiracy was well designed to play upon the weaknesses, selfishness, greed, cupidity and stupidity of the bulk of mankind.

Robison, in his PROOFS OF A CONSPIRACY sums up Weishaupt's Illuminist program, as follows:

> "In the lodges, death was declared eternal sleep; patriotism and loyalty were called narrow-minded prejudices incompatible with benevolence; . . . they meant to abolish laws which protected property accumulated by long-continued and successful industry; and to prevent future accumulations . . . they intended to root out all religion and ordinary morality . . . to break the bonds of domestic life by destroying veneration for marriage vows, and by taking the education of children out of the hands of parents."

These plans could only derive from a successful imposition on mankind of the organizational aspects of the conspiracy. This organization, modified to adapt it to American conditions are embodied in Clinton Roosevelt's SCIENCE OF GOVERNMENT. Direct derivatives of such organization are the administrative phases of Weishaupt's conspiracy. They are in effect the following essential measures:

1. Overthrow of existent governments and their replacement by a dictatorship of the conspirators.
2. Looting individuals and nations of their wealth through such devices as violence and war, capital and income taxes, confiscatory inheritance taxes, and eventually an end of private ownership of property, except at the hands of the conspirators who would then own all property and usurp the power that such ownership would yield.
3. Destruction of all religions, supplanting them with doctrines laid down by the conspirators.
4. Destruction of the family and supplanting its discipline by that of the dictators.
5. "Internationalism" that was required by the conspirators' scheme for control over "One World" — involving the outlawing of patriotism and the fostering of treason.

These aspects of the conspiracy were first widely broadcast, with the aid of Clinton Roosevelt and his Illuminist associates, by Heinrich Karl Marx, who as usual plagiarized them without even intimating the Weishaupt-Illuminist source.

THE RISE OF THE ILLUMINIST-SOCIALIST-COMMUNIST CONSPIRACY IN AMERICA

On July 16, 1782, at the Congress of Wilhelmsbad, an alliance was entered into by the Masonic Order and the Order of Illuminati which has had tremendous repercussions in world history. The two thousand lodges of the Order of Illuminati that had come into existence almost overnight, joined the lodges of the Masonic Order in a world-wide organization that claimed over three million members.

The Order of Illuminati started when the American Revolution was already under way, and therefore, played no significant part in it. However, before the colonies were united, the Constitution adopted, and our Republic established, fifteen lodges of the Order of Illuminati were established in the thirteen Colonies. In 1785 the Columbian Lodge of the Order of Illuminati was established in New York City. With it were identified Governor DeWitt Clinton, and later Clinton Roosevelt, Charles A. Dana and Horace Greeley. In 1786 there was established a lodge in Virginia, with which was identified Thomas Jefferson.

When the Order of Illuminati was exposed as a revolutionary conspiracy in Bavaria, and Weishaupt was attacked, Jefferson, an ardent Illuminist, defended Weishaupt as an "enthusiastic philanthropist."

The Order of Illuminati rapidly gained such influence in the Colonies that its members were able to force the adoption of the Order's insignia as the Great Seal of the United States of America. It can be found on the left side of the reverse of the one dollar silver certificates of the Treasury. Its eye mounted on a pyramid signifies the "all-spying eye" that was symbolic of Illuminism's terrorist espionage system (the counterpart of the Gestapo, the Ogpu and the NKVD and of the other cruel and brutal spy nets that Weishaupt's disciples have since adopted). Placing the symbol on the great Seal of the USA was a warning that the entire power of the Republic stood behind the very conspiracy that aimed to destroy it and threatened violence supported by terrorist espionage to those who opposed the conspirators. NOVUS ORDO SECLORUM — announces the "NEW DEAL", of Weishaupt's Illuminists. The date on the insignia and Seal base of the pyramid—MDCCLXXVI, or 1776—is not meant as the date of the Declaration of Independence which occurred in the same year, but is the date of the founding of Weishaupt's conspiracy, the Order of Illuminati. Never have revolutionary conspirators been more audacious or less suspected.

In Bavaria, as has been stated, the Order of Illuminati was exposed as a nefarious conspiracy and it was forced underground in 1785. In the United States, it continued to thrive and prosper in spite of numerous attacks from public platform and pulpit, as a subversive, counter-Revolutionary conspiracy that aimed to destroy our Government and Constitution. Among the attackers in 1798 were Rev. Jedediah Morse, President Timothy Dwight, of Yale University, and, to the chagrin of many modern Harvardites, David Tappan, a Harvard officer. In 1800, following some riots centering about activities of the Order in New York City and elsewhere, many Illuminist lodges went underground or completely merged with Masonic lodges.

The Columbian Lodge of the Order of Illuminati emerged into the open once again, as the Columbian Lodge of the Masonic Order about 1838. High in its ranks was Assemblyman Clinton Roosevelt, a descendant of Claes Martenszen van Rosenvelt and his wife Jannetje Samuels. Clinton R. is cousin of more than a dozen U. S. Presidents, including Theodore Roosevelt, Franklin Delano Roosesevelt, John and John Quincy Adams, James Madison, and Martin Van Buren, all members of the Roosevelt-Delano Dynasty (see the STRANGE DEATH OF FRANKLIN D. ROOSEVELT Chedney Press, 1948) that calls itself America's Royal Family.

The Dynasty owes to the Illuminist-Socialist-Communist "liberal" conspiracy its rise to power. Its continuance in power rests on its leadership in that conspiracy. Equally important is the control of the nominating machinery of both major political parties, and generally of all parties, held by the Roosevelt-Delano Dynasty since the founding of our Republic. This has permitted them to mock and deride the nation's pretense to self-rule.

Cousin John Adams was a founder of the Federalist Party antecedent of the Republican Party, and from its beginning, he gained control of its nominating machinery for his kinsmen of the Dynasty. Cousin Martin Van Buren, as running mate of Andrew Jackson, was one of the founders of the Democratic Party. He gained control of the nominating machinery of the Democratic Party for his Dynastic kinsmen; and they have retained it ever since. Since then the Dynasty has gained control of the nominating machinery of every new party that came into being, whether Liberal, Labor, Communist, Socialist, Bull Moose, Whig, or Republican.

Traditionally, they have shown no loyalty except to their selfish interests. No religion or party has ever held their adherence. Almost every third party movement in our history has been launched by a disgruntled member of the Dynasty seeking to assert his claim to public office.

On October 29, 1835, Clinton Roosevelt and his powerful associates and Illuminist fellow conspirators, who were members of Tammany Hall, undertook to take over control of Tammany and impress its organization into the furtherance of their plot. The way had been prepared for this move by the agitation stirred up by a British female Illuminist, Frances ("Fanny") Wright, who came to this country in 1829 to give a series of lectures at Masonic Hall. She advocated the entire Illuminist program of her auxiliary of the Order of Illuminati (see p. 73) including Communism made more palatable by the label of "equal opportunity and equal rights," atheism, emancipation of women and free love. She had won a large following among the rabble, who, organized as the "Workingmen's" Party, had polled 6,000 of the 20,000 votes in the election in 1829, had elected a member of Legislature and had defeated the Tammany candidate. Clinton Roosevelt and his fellow Illuminati undertook to capitalize on the groundwork done for them by the licentious feminist emissary of the Order from abroad.

The boss of Tammany was prepared for the move, and had arranged to have the gaslights in the Hall turned off, so as to leave the conspirators in darkness and close the meeting before they could carry out their scheme. But the conspirators came prepared for the maneuver. They came armed with the matches then in use, the "Loco-Foco" matches, and relit the gas lights so that the meeting could proceed. They thus earned for themselves the name "Loco-Foco Party."

The "Loco Focos" posed as champions of the "new social order," the New Deal and of "equal rights." They prated of their intent "to kick the moneylenders out of the temple" and were opposed to monopolies. Masked by these "noble and worthy" causes that appealed to the moronic mentality of the "peasants," the Illuminati of Loco Foco undertook to attain the dictatorship objectives laid down by Adam Weishaupt. It is noteworthy that in their initial program, Roosevelt and his crew pretended that they were seeking to uphold the Constitution. In his "THE SCIENCE OF GOVERNMENT" published shortly thereafter, Roosevelt frankly urged the gutting and abandonment of the Constitution, which he compared with a "sinking ship" (see p. 88).

Roosevelt's Loco Focos did not succeed in their initial effort to impress Tammany Hall into their conspiracy. In the following year Roosevelt and his fellow Illuminati organized a "third party," an old and confirmed habit of the Roosevelt conspirators when they fail to get their wish, at a meeting held in their Masonic Hall. They nominated themselves as the candidates of the new party, the Whigs. Following the "bipartisan" device dictated by Weishaupt and now a familiar pattern of the conspirators, Roosevelt sought and obtained for himself and his crew the nominations of the Democratic Party at its Utica convention held on September 15, 1836. They thus aligned both the Whig and the Democratic Parties as direct agencies of the Illuminist-Communist conspiracy. "BIPARTISANSHIP" is SYNONYMOUS WITH THE ILLUMINIST-COMMUNIST CONSPIRACY.

The U. S., thus had what was in effect, if not in name, a Communist dictatorship party fully three quarters of a century before Russia dreamed of Communism; and more than a decade before Moses Mordecai Marx Levy, alias Heinrich Karl

Marx, and Engels, sought to duplicate in Europe the successes of their fellow conspirators in the U. S. A.

Emboldened by success, Roosevelt published in 1841, THE SCIENCE OF GOVERNMENT FOUNDED ON NATURAL LAW. It embodies, as stated, Adam Weishaupt's pattern of organization of a "One World", United Nations dictatorship as a blueprint of the "New Deal," or "New Social Order" that Roosevelt planned to impose on the U. S. A., as a part of the "international" conspiracy. The plan called for the gradual emasculation and eventual abandonment of the Constitution as a "sinking ship." The Roosevelt book, in many of its passages was quite patently a translation of Weishaupt's German and obviously plagiarized, with slight modifications for American adaptation. In much the same manner Moses Mordecai Marx Levy, alias Karl Marx seven years later, with aid from America, plagiarized the blueprint of the complementary and derivative administrative aspects of Weishaupt's scheme and published it as his COMMUNIST MANIFESTO. The two publications taken together constitute the whole of Weishaupt's scheme for imposing a Communist dictatorship on the world.

It was no accident that the substance of the entire Communist blueprint of Weishaupt's Illuminati was thus published internationally. World subjugation is of necessity an international affair. The "internationalism" dictated by Weishaupt and stressed by his disciple, Roosevelt, is essentially a conspiracy, treason. Members of the conspiracy are required to infiltrate their governments and to help their fellow Illuminist conspirators extend their infiltration to the point of taking over control of the governments. They are required to foster dissension between groups within nations and war between nations, for the purpose of weakening existent governments. For the same purpose they are required to bankrupt their governments and people by profligate waste and excessive taxation; and to betray their countries into the hands of their enemies. Above all else, they must place the wealth and resources of their countries at the disposal of the master conspirators for furthering the conspiracy in other lands.

Roosevelt and his Illuminist henchmen carefully heeded Weishaupt's "internationalist" teachings. As soon as their efforts were crowned with success at home, they undertook to foster the conspiracy in Europe. Without their support, Illuminism might have died in Europe. Their instigation and support made possible the 1848 revolution in Europe and the subsequent stimulus to the conspiracy.

Without the Loco Foco, Illuminist-Communist activities of Clinton Roosevelt and his clan, Karl Marx would have remained an obscure, demented German agitator. Charles A. Dana and Horace Greeley gave Karl Marx and his plagiarized Communist Manifesto the international audience that was necessary to give them significance, by employing their fellow-Illuminist Marx as correspondent and columnist for their New York Tribune. As related by Willam Hale in his biography, HORACE GREELEY, Dana excelled himself in spreading the Illuminist-Communist ideas parroted by Marx and Engels (his ghostwriter) by plagiarizing parts of their articles and publishing the propaganda as his editorials (p. 155). Without this early American support of Marx's Illuminism-Communism, his rise would have been as impossible as the later rise of Lenin, Trotzky and Stalin would have been without American support in the first and second Russian Revolution.

ROOSEVELT'S ILLUMINIST-COMMUNIST NEW DEAL PROGRAM

Roosevelt proclaimed his adherence to Adam Weishaupt's Illuminism in the very title of his book. For though Weishaupt ordered that all arts, sciences and religions should be abolished he undertook to replace them by the "social(ist) science of government" propounded by himself and pronounced by him to be the only true science. Weishaupt also dictated that it must be founded on "natural law" which he alleged is the only true law. Plagiarist Roosevelt followed suit, and wrote THE SCIENCE OF GOVERNMENT FOUNDED ON NATURAL LAW.

Weishaupt ruled that

> "The Superiors of the Order (of Illuminati) are to be regarded as the most perfect and enlightened of men; they must not even permit any doubts of their infallibility."

Roosevelt starts his SCIENCE OF GOVERNMENT with a preface that is a testy dissertation on his superior wisdom and infallibility, that he orders shall not be questioned; and he demands that the whole world acquiesce in it. He scorns any pretense of modesty in his self-praise. He condemns his critics in advance for their ignorance and stupidity in failing to recognize his omniscience. And he demands that praise shall be heaped upon him from all corners of the world. This attitude is the familiar "Papa knows best" attitude that is so characteristic of the Roosevelt-Delano Dynasty and their fellow conspirators.

Copying Weishaupt, Roosevelt next proceeds to "divide to rule", by inciting class warfare, the most demoralizing form of civil war. He acknowledges that control and manipulation of money is the root of all the evils which he decries. But instead of attacking this root, which is the very device that he and his fellow Illuminists plan to use for the enslavement of mankind, he vaguely and fleetingly suggests "kicking the moneylenders (who happen to be he and his kinsmen) out of the temple." He commiserates with the "producer, the forgotten man." He professes that he feels so sorry for laborers that he wishes to regiment them and enslave them, on an *"international"* basis. The power thus gained he plans to use to wage war on the workers' fellow victims of the dishonest monetary system, on their employers. He thus plans to usurp their property, regiment them under his dictation, and distribute their wealth — in the direction of himself and his fellow conspirators. He plans to emasculate and destroy the Constitution, which he likens to a "sinking ship," to make way for a dictatorship of his own devising. This dictatorship and the slavery that it entails, he labels a "new social order."

Roosevelt's dictatorship program is identical with the organization program prescribed by Weishaupt for the carrying out of his Illuminist conspiracy for world control. Labor organization, the control, regimentation and subversion of the "masses", was conceived by Weishaupt as a means of attaining power over the state as well as a device for financing his conspiracy. And virtually all labor organization since then has continued in control of the conspirators, vicious exploiters of labor who pose as "labor leaders." The conspirators systematically take advantage of such eras of high employment and prosperity as their conspiracy permits, to loot the workers by dues and assessments, on the pretense that they have provided the higher wages that prosperity and a high level of employment have brought about — in spite of their malign, divisive activities. As a result, organized labor has been a captive of the subversive conspirators for more than a century. In their pose of "friends of labor" and "labor leaders" they have cunningly used labor as their prime weapon in the war which they wage on the community, year in and year out, to enslave it together with labor.

In the SCIENCE OF GOVERNMENT Roosevelt blueprints the regimentation of every phase of the community life in the pattern that has become so familiar to us, in the so-called "New Deal" of his kinsman, President Franklin Delano Roosevelt. FDR and his fellow conspirators followed the blueprint of his kinsman so closely, that the organization of the New Deal's NRA can be recognized clearly in the diagram published by Clinton in the SCIENCE OF GOVERNMENT FOUNDED ON NATURAL LAW. But present-day Roosevelts pretend they have no knowledge of cousin Clinton or his book.

Clinton Roosevelt's Loco Foco activities spelled the conversion of the Democratic Party to the support of the Illuminist-Socialist-Communist conspiracy. "Bipartisanship" resulted in the contamina- of the opposition with the same affection. This has resulted in making Illuminist-Socialist-Communist doctrines and policies an integral part of American political thought and life.

Thus it is fully understandable that the Kremlin has always trusted the Roosevelts. It was quite mete that the USSR was prepared to honor the American dynasty that did so much to make possible its rise, in the person of Eleanor Roosevelt. They offered to send an official plane to meet her at Helsinki, when she announced her intent to visit the Soviets in July, 1954. This trip was part of a plan to align the subversive, Communist vote behind the candidacy of her two sons, Kiss-And-Tell Jimmy, and Love-Em-Sock-Em-Leave-Em Franklin who were prepared to execute a pincer movement on the nation from two continent-separated, Communist-infested sections of the country, in the furtherance of the Illuminist inspired conspiracy. "Queen" Eleanor spared herself the agony of sojourn in the conspirators' Soviet "paradise" by making demands on her prospective hosts with which they could not comply. But it would be quite fitting that the Soviets bury her in the Kremlin in recognition of the role that she and her ancestors played in making possible the rise of Communism and the USSR. It would make many folks on the side of the Atlantic happy.

It was quite in keeping with the character of the Roosevelts that Eleanor Roosevelt denied, in a letter to me, any knowledge of her "distinguished" kinsman Clinton Roosevelt, the author of the New Deal aspects of the conspiracy that was faithfully carried out by Cousin Franklin D. How well the Roosevelts are aware of the progress of the conspiracy is evidenced by the prediction made by, or with the acquiescence of, Theodore Roosevelt in the late 1890's, that is cited by Owen Wister in his ROOSEVELT, The Story Of A Friendship (MacMillan Co 1930, p. 51) as follows:

> "How long do you give the government at Washington to last?" I asked (Theodore) Roosevelt and (Cabot) Lodge as we sat lunching.
>
> Those two students and writers — and makers — of history, well versed in the causes which

have led to the downfall of empires, kingdoms and republics that have had their day and gone into the night, were both silent for a moment; then one of them said:

"ABOUT FIFTY YEARS."

Which of the two set this limit, I do not recall; I remember only that the other did not contradict him.

Clinton Roosevelt, son of Elbert Cornelius Roosevelt and Margaret R., was born October 3, 1804; and he died a bachelor at the ripe old age of ninety three, on August 1, 1898. His entire life was dedicated to the furthering of the Illuminist-Socialist-Communist dictatorship conspiracy, the "new social order" that now parades as the New Deal. The persistence of his political activity and of his propagandist zeal is attested to by a long series of pamphlets of which a number can be found in the main New York City Library, which catalogues the following:

1. The mode of protecting domestic industry by operating on the currency. 1833
2. The mode of protecting domestic industry consistent with the desires both of the South and the North — by operating on the currency. 1833
3. On the paradox of political economy in co-existence of excessive production and excessive population.
4. The Science Of Government Founded On Natural Law. 1841.
5. Opinion on the right of conscience and property in Trinity Church to King's farm and garden, and the Dominie Bogardus bowery, and also in the rights in Collegiate Reformed Dutch Church to trust estates of Steenwig Harpending By Lex (Pseudonym) Copyright by Clinton Roosevelt. 1865
6. Collection of works by Clinton Roosevelt. 1889

In the Library of Congress are the following additional items:

7. Proposition of a new system of political economy.
8. Charges and arguments against Thomas Eubank, Commissioner of Patents.

THE ILLUMINIST-SOCIALIST-COMMUNIST DICTATORSHIP CONSPIRACY IN AMERICA TODAY

The Illuminist-Socialist-Communist dictatorship conspiracy to which Clinton Roosevelt dedicated his life is an accomplished fact in Soviet Russia and its satellites. In the United States and the so-called "Free World," it falls little short of complete success. The rapid attainment by the conspirators of their objective within the past fifty years contrasts sharply with the slow progress of their plot in the century and quarter prior. It was made possible by support of the greatest fortune and power that the world has ever known—by the Rockefellers. Their interest and involvement in the curiously traitorous "United" Nations, "One World" set-up is a matter of public record. It is less widely known that Alger Hiss was their agent in engineering it.

A number of reasons can be discerned why the Rockefellers would find it expedient to foster a "One World" dictatorship. First and foremost, exposure of the gangsterism, racketeering and brigandage of Rockefellers, at the turn of the century, had created a motive of fear of the resentment of the world. Second, was resentment at the resultant verdict handed down by Judge Keneshaw Landis in 1907, that ordered the dissolution of the Standard Oil Co., that had been the evil life-work of John D. Rockefeller; and it was only partly avenged by the 1907 panic precipitated several weeks later. Third, was the fear that some one would arise who would be more unscrupulous and ruthless than themselves and who would rob them of their wealth by the same methods they had used. Fourth, was the running battle that the Rockefellers and their Standard Oil associates had waged for decades on their chief competitors, the Royal Dutch Company, for the control of the oil reserves and markets of the world, and more particularly, of the British Empire and British spheres of influence, from which Standard Oil Co. had been excluded.

The most important source of oil for the European market, that was the bone of contention, was that from the Russian oilfields, especially the Baku fields; the most important untapped oil reserve, Saudi Arabia. Both were in the British "sphere of influence" and controlled by British interests that shut out Rockefellers' Standard Oil Co. Royal Dutch had a monopolistic concession that they refused to share with the Standard Oil Co. And the Czarist regime refused to cancel the concession. This meant that the Rockefeller interests could not gain access to Baku oil except by one of three devices: either by destroying the Czarist regime by revolution, or by creating a breach between the Czarist regime and the Royal Dutch group, or by both. And they could gain access to Saudi Arabian oil only by destroying the British Empire, by breaking its hold over Arabia and the Near East, or by both.

For the purpose of attaining these objectives and of "ensuring security," Weishaupt's dictatorship conspiracy with the multitude of adherents it had gained during centuries, was ideally adapted. How well Rockefeller and his advisers were aware of it, already has been made clear in connection with Occasional Letter No. 1 in which Rockefeller and his almoner stated the purpose of his "educational philanthrophy," the General Education Board (v. page 17).

Illustrative of how closely the Rockefellers have followed the Weishaupt pattern, "court minorities" and "divide and rule" is the not so widely known initial purpose of the GEB. This Rockefeller "philanthropy" was originally planned solely for the education of negroes according to Allan Nevins in his official biography, authorized by the family (p. 483), This plan was abandoned when it was realized that brain-washing the balance of the populace would necessitate the setting up of a multiplicity of foundations.

But the Rockefellers are, and always have been, the most influential advocates of assimilation and "homogenization" of the negroes by intermarriage and other processes—on the part of the "peasants"; but they themselves have very carefully refrained from giving an example by leading the way and intermarrying with negroes — except unintentionally . The Rockefellers are the all-powerful supporters of the FEPC and of negro organizations such as the Urban League (of which Winthrop Rockefeller is an officer) and others, that foster and promote negro dominance and Communism among the negroes. Ralph J. Bunche is the top negro protege and agent of the Rockefellers in the furtherance among the blacks of the Illuminist-Socialist-Communist conspiracy, whether it be among the civil colored folks of Southern U.S.A. or the savage Mau Maus of Kenya. So powerful is the protection given by the Rockefeller interests to Bunche, that when former-Communist informers working for the FBI exposed Ralph J. Bunche as a fellow Communist, they were ousted from the FBI and threatened with prosecution and persecuted in the Weishaupt-Gestapo tradition. Bunche was "cleared" of the charges in secret "hearings" conducted by the conspirators' agents. And then Bunche was promoted to the third ranking position in the UN, the conspirators' top "One World" agency.

Since the first decade of this century, the Rockefellers have made no secret of the fact that they are the real patrons and bosses of Communism and of other form of totalitarianism in the pattern of Weishaupt. They have openly published in the reports of their foundations — the General Education Board, the Laura Spelman Rockefeller Memorial, and the Rockefeller Foundation, as well as the other individual organizations of the "Philanthropic" Foundation Trust, which they have set up — the details of their support of the Illuminist-Socialist-Communist conspiracy. Some of this support is camouflaged as a subsidy of Weishaupt's *social(ist) science* whose devotees, willy-nilly, are trained as adherents and agents of the Illuminist-Socialist-Communist conspiracy; and since they can only "succeed" in making a living by furthering the dictatorship conspiracy, they are all of them, with very few exceptions, traitors. Through these Rockefeller "philanthropies", the "social sciences" are now being taught all children in the country's school system starting in the lowest grades.

Two such undertakings as overthrowing the Czarist regime in Russia and destroying the British

Empire might daunt a less ruthless spirit. But it was taken in stride by John D. Rockefeller. Indeed, he made it a phase of a greater and more grandiose scheme — a super-Napoleonic plan to take over the entire world by cunning, crafty pitting of one nation against another, of one half of the world against the other, in continuous warfare in commerce, industry and on the battlefield, that enormously enriches himself, while impoverishing the world until prostrate and utterly exhausted, all will fall completely under his dominion as "One World" — Rockefeller's World, the U.N.

Through their banker, Jacob Schiff, of Kuhn Loeb & Co., the Rockefeller agencies were instrumental in agitating, fomenting and financing the first, unsuccessful attempt at a Revolution in Russia, for the purpose of taking control of the Baku oilfields from their competitors, the Royal Dutch Co. Jacob Schiff, as a Jew, served another purpose in the conspiracy. The principals of the Royal Dutch are the British Crown, the Dutch Crown, and a group of Jewish families — the Isaacs, Samuels, Rothschilds and Sassoons. With Jew Jacob Schiff as red herring and front, the impression was created that the Jews were attempting to overthrow the Czarist regime. This device was intended to create a breach between the Russian Government and the Royal Dutch group that might result in the cancellation of the latter's concessions.

The impression of a Jewish conspiracy against the Czar was fortified by the simultaneous publication of the teachings of Adam Weishaupt (the renegade Jesuit) for the Priestcraft degree of the Order of Illuminati, translated into Russia under the name of THE PROTOCOLS OF ZION. There was more than a mere coincidence in the timing of this publication and the Revolution. It was well designed to make it appear that the Russian Revolution was but one phase of an attempt of *the Jews* to take over control of the world and attain the objectives laid down by Weishaupt and furthered by Rockefeller. Malefactors have always found it wise to establish an alibi or to set up a "fall guy." In this instance as in so many others, the always suspect Jews served the purpose, primarily because they lack the cunning and perspicacity to realize that they are being "used."

Henry Ford, in this instance, as in others, also was used as a dumb pawn by the Rockefeller interests in spreading this false propaganda, and to "take the rap" for it. The Ford Foundation, which through the control of the Treasury Department has been taken over by the agents of the Rockefeller interests, is being used by them for the same purpose. The Ford family will be extremely fortunate if they are not robbed completely of their enterprise by the conspirators.

Through Jacob Schiff, the conspirators financed the efforts of Lenin, Trotsky, Stalin and their criminal crew of followers of Adam Weishaupt, in the Russian Revolution of 1905, most of the action of which took place in the Baku oilfields. When the revolution failed, its leaders were whisked away to Switzerland to bide their time for another opportunity. The sources of the funds, that supported them and their activities in that expensive country, was the same. Grants of Rockefeller's General Education Board can be traced to the revolutionary conspiracy.

The net result of 1905 revolutionary phase of the conspiracy was massacres, or "Progroms", of the Jews in various sections of Russia and Poland. These merely served to lend credibility and support to the charges that it was the Jews who were seeking to overthrow the Czar; and they served as a perfect cloak for the conspiracy.

The failure of the revolution necessitated a new plan. Offers were made to Kaiser Wilhelm to finance the building of the Berlin-to-Bagdad Railway by Germany. This meant that the Near East would be lost to the British as a "sphere of influence"; and its control would be in the hands of the Germans. The price of the deal was that control of the Arabian oilfields would be given to Standard Oil Co. Thus was World War I engineered by the Rockefeller interests.

In the midst of the war, at about the time of Verdun, the British awoke to the realization that they could not win the war without American aid;

that the British Empire must bow to the Rockefeller Empire, or succumb. The British offered the Rockefeller interests that they would permit their puppet king of Saudi Arabia, Ibn Saud, to give them a concession to the Saudi Arabian oil fields if they would force the U.S.A. to enter the war, finance and fight it. The conspirators distrusted their partners, the Germans. They accepted the British deal. Then they turned about and had the German General Staff transport Lenin, Trotsky & Co. through Germany to the Russian border; and provided them with hundreds of millions of counterfeit ten ruble notes printed by an American bank note company, and paid for by the conspirators, with which to buy the votes of the soldiers and sailors in favor of the version of the Weishaupt dictatorship conspiracy that now goes by the name of Communism. It is the height of irony that the Russian people were bribed with counterfeit currency and duped by equally counterfeit propaganda into selling themselves into murderous serfdom. They sold the freedom that was theirs for the taking, for less than "a mess of potage" — for worthless counterfeits, for scraps of paper, and false promises of "security."

Once risen to power, "idealist" Lenin double-crossed his bosses. He turned over to Harry F. Sinclair, a protege of President Harding, and his associates who included Theodore Roosevelt Jr., a monopoly of all Russian oilfields. This was the prize for which the Rockefeller interests had schemed for decades and had brought about the extermination of millions of the human race to secure. Through the Teapot Dome deal, which they engineered for the purpose, Sinclair was jailed and broken. *President Harding died suddenly of poisoning.* The Rockefeller interests sent an officer of theirs, Dodge, to Russia to try to force Lenin to obey orders and turn over to them the deal he had made with Sinclair. *Lenin refused and he died suddenly of poisoning.* Stalin was placed in control of Russia. Directly thereafter, in 1926, he entered into a deal with the Rockefellers and their interests, which gave them control of Russian oil in the world market, and protected their fabulous Saudi Arabian holdings that the Russians could seize at any time they wish. Those Saudi Arabian holdings have been the keystone of the conspiracy and of world affairs since. They have furnished the Weishaupt-conceived conspiracy with foundation of solid wealth, and the power derived therefrom, that previously it had lacked. World dictatorship was made thereby not merely a possibility, but also a necessity — for the Rockefeller interests.

The terms of the deal made with Stalin have never been published. But they can easily be surmised from the subsequent course of events, and from statements made and published by Rockefeller agents, to be as follows:

1. Division of the world between Stalin and the Rockefeller Empire, with delivery of all of Asia to the Soviets, except Saudi Arabia.
2. Delivery of oil produced in Saudi Arabia, or its equivalent, to the Soviets, at the expense of American taxpayers.
3. Establishment of a "Popular Front" government (dominated by Reds) in the United States of America.
4. Recognition of Russia.
5. Industrialization of Russia — at the expense of American taxpayers.
6. Rearmament of Russia — at the expense of American taxpayers.
7. Control of surplus Russian oil by the Rockefeller interests.
8. Soviet acquiescence and support of the Rockefeller interests in the development of Saudi Arabia.

The consummation of the initial phases of the deal was exultantly published in Rockefeller's official journal, the New York Times, on March 27, 1926. And on the following day the Times announced that Rockefeller's publicity man Ivy Lee had begun to lay the foundation for the recognition of Russia and the carrying out of other phases of the conspiracy. In May 1927, Ivy Lee went to Russia for ten days to confer, on behalf of his employers, with Stalin and Radek and to learn their wishes and ideas. On his return he wrote a book entitled USSR — AN

ENIGMA that was privately printed by his employers and distributed to henchmen and agents in the Council of Foreign Relations and in the Federal Government. In it Ivy Lee announced that "internationalism," which is the keynote of the Illuminist-Socialist-Communist conspiracy of Adam Weishaupt, had become the program of his Rockefeller employers. In his subsequently published correspondence, Lee also announcd it was their intention to comply with the conditions laid down by Bolshevik Radek for creating in the U. S. sentiment for recognition of Russia and for carrying out the other terms of the Rockefeller-Stalin deal — an end to the period of prosperity in the U. S. Thus, with the launching of the Rockefeller-Soviet Axis, did the Rockefeller crew openly put on an ultra-intensive campaign for promotion of the Weishaupt program.

The same Ivy Lee served his master in another phase of the conspiracy in 1933, when he was employed by them to advise Hitler and Goebbels on propaganda and publicity methods, and to advise the Nazi Party on the rearmament of Germany. This was occasioned by British bad faith in refusing to permit the Rockefeller-Standard Oil interests to develop the Saudi Arabia oilfields for which they had obtained concessions. The same group induced Mussolini to invade Ethiopia so as to obtain for the Rockefeller interests control of the oilfields in the Fafan Valley of the Harrar Province of Abyssinia, which Haile Selassie, under British pressure, refused to permit them to develop; and which they now hold. They were the moving spirits behind the Stalin-Hitler entente. And they engineered World War II to get a free rein in the development of Saudi Arabia by crushing the British Empire, to make good on their deal with Stalin, and to attain the One World, United Nations objective of the conspirators.

The Rockefeller interests made good on the setting up of a "Popular Front" government in the U.S.A. in 1933, in the form of the Roosevelt regime. Clinton Roosevelt's kinsman, Franklin D. was a natural figurehead sanctioned by family tradition to front for Weishaupt's Illuminist - Socialist-Communist conspiracy. His selection was no accident, but was a part of the conspirator's scheme of hereditary transmission of key roles in the conspiracy. This is a device for preparing us "peasants" for hereditary dictator-rulers, that was decreed by Adam Weishaupt.

Directly after Franklin D. Roosevelt's inauguration, the conspirators proceeded to try to inflict on the nation every remaining phase of Clinton Roosevelt's Illuminist blueprint for destroying our Constitution and Government — on the pretense of establishing a "new social order", or "New Deal," as they ironically labeled it. They promptly placed the insignia of the Order of Illuminati, in the form of the Great Seal of the U. S., on the currency, thus exulting brazenly in the attainment of the goal of their conspiracy — "Novus Ordo Seclorum", the Latin version of "New Deal." This should have served as a warning to investigators of un-American activities and to hunters of Communists that the entire power of the U. S. is dedicated to the subversive conspiracy; and that they might expect to be hounded, persecuted and destroyed by the conspirators' terroristic espionage agency—their "Gestapo". But the naive, uninformed patriots knew it not!

Under the pretense of ending the depression, the conspirators carried Weishaupt's plan of government control of the banking system (at their hands) one step further than they had dared to do at the time of the adoption of their Federal Reserve System.

Under the pretense of economy, loyal civil servants were discharged, and shortly thereafter, they were replaced by an endless horde of henchmen of the conspirators who had been indoctrinated in the school system that had been converted by the Rockefeller "educational philanthropies" into the conspirator's training schools for subversives. It is safe to say that well over one million Communist, fellow travelers and subversives — Illuminist followers of Adam Weishaupt — were planted permanently on the Federal payroll in the decade that followed; and most of them still remain there, in every branch of the Government from the President and his executive assistants, the Associate Judges of the Supreme Court, the Congress, down to the lowest bracket of bureaucrats. The Martin Dieses, Hamilton Fishes, Parnell Thomases and Joseph McCarthys could expose a new Communist every day in the year for the next thousand years, and still not exhaust the roll of Communists firmly planted on the Federal payroll. This serves to emphasize the sham of the investigators of un-American activities who have deliberately refused to expose the top bosses and financeers of the Illuminist-Communist dictatorship conspiracy — the Rockefeller interests.

The conspirators promptly proceeded to carry out every phase of the Weishaupt-Roosevelt scheme. Deliberately intensifying and prolonging the depression that they had precipitated, facilitated the process. Weishaupt's program of control of the banking system by the conspirators was promoted by closing down the nation's banks; putting out of existence all banks not controlled by the conspirators, no matter how solvent; and subsidizing all banks controlled by them, no matter how insolvent. Also the Government was put in the banking business, as an aid to the conspirators, through a multitude of agencies. Weishaupt's plan of government ownership of industry was carried out by launching the government in an endless array of industries.

A beginning was made in the process of the elimination of private ownership of property by all other than the conspirators, by the institution of a progressive, confiscatory system of taxation that was avowedly designed for the prime purpose of "distribution of wealth" — a euphuism for the conspirators' seizure of wealth through the agency of the Government. "Taking the nation off the gold standard," the conspirators robbed the citizenry of their gold by compelling them to turn it over to their private corporation, the Federal Reserve Bank. When the author remonstrated in a letter published in the New York Times, that confiscation of wealth for the benefit of private interests is not only un-Constitutional, but is also thievery, the conspirators covered up their trail with the second Roosevelt "gold order" that supposedly required the Federal Reserve Bank to turn its gold over to the U. S. Treasury. Actually this is not a fact. For, the private stockholder-controlled national banks were given ten thousand dollar notes redeemable by them in gold. This is a closely guarded secret. It makes the gold held by the Treasury actually the property of the conspirators, as private stockholders of national bank stock. The conspirators alone have been permitted to withdraw the gold from the Treasury and to profit enormously from international shipments of gold and from gold revaluations internationally engineered by them for their profit.

Intimidation of the nation has been a by-product of the un-Constitutional device adopted for the confiscation of wealth—of the Federal Income Tax administered by the Internal Revenue Division of the Treasury Department. Rank corruption and favoritism in the arbitrary, bureaucratic administration of the confiscatory income and inheritance taxes and an elaborate system of espionage have made it a device for rewarding favorites of the conspirators and robbing and jailing their foes. It has also reduced a large section of the nation to marginal existence by wiping out the possibilities of savings and reserves and made others wholely dependent upon the bounty of the conspirators to the taxpayers by way of welfare doles, unemployment insurance and the other devices of the "Social *Security*" Administration. This intimidation was intensified by the style of vindictive persecution and purging of adversaries, just as was dictated by Adam Weishaupt, for terrorizing opposition. The Communist nature of the income tax is stressed by one of the few patriotic Americans in public life—Governor P. B. Lee, of Utah.

Regimentation and browbeating of the nation into submission has been attempted and effected through numerous devices. First and foremost of these devices are the generally corrupt and subversive private labor unions dominated by the conspirators and their agents. They rob workers of freedom of employment that is one of the freedoms supposedly assured by the Constitution and the Bill of Rights. They levy a special private tax on workers for the privilege of working, under the pretense of "protecting" them, and subject them to threat and violence, as well as with loss of employment if they fail to pay the tax. They blackmail industry into payments to their dictator "leaders" of huge sums of money for the supposed "welfare" of their victim-members. They engage with immunity in monopolies in restraint of trade exercised through the device of strikes which bar workers from earning their wages and deny to employers use of their own property. At the whim of so-called "leaders," they frequently violate public interest and endanger public health, in "general" strikes. They not infrequently engage in a wide assortment of illegal and criminal activities. And they systematically price their vassals out of employment, bringing on unemployment on vast scales, and then loot and abandon them to the tender mercies of the community. To all of this the conspirators, with their New Deal, force the workers of the nation to submit, when improvement in industry provided them with employment.

The most significant consequence for the conspirators of the control of labor, through regimentation in unions, has been utterly unsuspected by the community at large. IT IS THE FACT THAT LABOR UNIONIZATION IS AN ALTERNATIVE DEVICE FOR EFFECTING A REVOLUTION AND MAKING UNION BOSSES DICTATORS. The conspirators have placed themselves as labor leaders, and their unions, that supposedly protect the workers, above all law—civil or criminal. This power they have used to blackmail the workers, industry and the community, until they have reached the point of mercilessly looting all and taking over control of industry, commerce, banking and the government. Thus John L. Lewis now is one of the more powerful bankers in the country through his success in blackmailing the coal and other industries by such devices as the "welfare" fund. But of even higher significance is the success of one of the nation's arch-plotters, Institute of Maxim Gorki, Moscow-trained, Walter Reuther, president of the CIO, who is gaining such dominance in the industrial and political structure of the U.S.A., that he has become an actual boss of the nation's political scene. According to Victor Riesel, he now can reasonably aspire to make himself

President of the U.S.A., with the support of his fellow plotters and the Rockefellers. Walter Reuther and his brother Victor openly announced in letters from Moscow and in articles published on their return, that their role and objective in gaining control of American Labor is Sovietization of the U.S.A. In short, through the control of labor the conspirators have come within striking distance of carrying out the Illuminist-Socialist-Communist conspiracy of Weishaupt's in the U.S.A. This could not occur without Rockefeller support.

Other devices for regimenting the nation, intimidating and forcing it into submission are the WPA, the CCC, conscription into the armed services and universal military training. These all conform to the Weishaupt-Roosevelt, Illuminist-Communist pattern.

Most striking has been the conspirators' success in the field of semantics — in making the word "freedom" synonymous with "serfdom."

In the effort to impose Clinton Roosevelt's modification of the Weishaupt plan, by regimenting industry into the NRA, the conspirators were defeated by the courage and the initiative of a small group of employers. The NRA was declared un-Constituional in the "sick chicken" verdict of a Supreme Court that was not yet fully packed by the conspirators.

Undaunted by this setback, the conspirators deliberately engineered World War II to enable them to get around the Constitution by forcing a regimentation of industry under the dictatorial wartime power that they usurped. It is a matter of record that the conspirators involved the U. S. in the war long before Congress declared war; and that the Rockefellers financed through their Institute of Pacific Relations (which is a Rockefeller-Soviet, subversive agency) the Communist Richard Sorge spy ring that induced the Japs to attack the U. S. at Pearl Harbor instead of attacking Rockefeller's ally Russia, as the Japanese high command originally planned. By the Pearl Harbor attack, Congress was forced to declare war.

At Yalta, Rockefeller's agent trusted by Stalin, Alger Hiss, made a deal that ratified once again the original Rockefeller-Stalin deal of 1926. Meanwhile, Roosevelt's double posed for pictures with "Uncle Joe." The organization of the United Nations, a fruition of Adam Weishaupt's "internationalist," "One World" dictatorship scheme, ensued with agent Alger Hiss carrying out the betrayal of the U.S.A. and of the world, as planned by the conspirators. The Korean War, with its deliberate forcing of the U.S.A. into a humiliating, disaster-ridden defeat by a thirty-second rate power, planned by the conspirators, was a cunningly arranged phase of the Yalta deal. Ironic indeed was the pretense of the conspirators in the top echelons of the U. S. government of attempting to avoid the war and defeat that they so treasonously schemed. The entire recent history of the U. S. as planned by the conspirators is redolent of the ruthlessness, brutality and criminality of Adam Weishaupt, and his disciples Roosevelt and Marx. The Illuminist-Socialist-Communist conspiracy is well on its way to enslaving a duped world, thanks to the Rockefeller dominated "Philanthropic" Foundation Trust.

From the very beginning, Rockefeller's so-called "philanthropies" have been dedicated to furthering the Illuminist-Socialist-Communist dictatorship conspiracy, to the utter exclusion of any other social or political cause. The Rockefeller Foundation was denied a charter by Congress, in 1910, 1911 and 1912, in spite of the political power of Rockefeller's agents in Congress who included John D. Rockefeller Jr.'s father-in-law, Senator Nelson Aldrich, because the purposes of the "philanthropies" were widely known to be a conspiracy to subvert our government and destroy our Constitution. Senator Chamberlain, of Oregon, clearly stated this fact in a speech made on the floor of the Senate, on March 26, 1917, as follows:

> "The Carnegie-Rockefeller influence is bad. In two generations they can change the minds of the people to make them conform to the cult (conspiracy) of Rockefeller, or to the cult (conspiracy) of Carnegie, rather than the fundamental principles of American democracy."

Time has proved Senator Chamberlain to be one of

the sagest of prophets. For already, his prophecy has been more than completely fulfilled.

Senator Chamberlain's differentiation of the cults of Rockefeller and Carnegie was his only error. For since 1905, the Rockefellers have controlled the Carnegie "philanthropies" and converted them to their purpose. Also they have managed, through their control of the Government and the Treasury Department, to usurp control of all foundations that they regard as worthwhile controlling, including the largest of them all, the Ford Foundation. The Rockefellers have merged all the foundations into a "Philanthropic" Foundation Trust, which is dedicated to carrying out the Weishaupt-Rockefeller program, a "One World" dictatorship.

So important is their "Philanthropic" Foundation Trust to the Rockefellers, that they have thrown all of their tremendous power and wealth into blocking any exposure of it by committees of Congress. Congressman Cox died before the investigation of foundations by his committee got under way. Congressman Carroll Reece became strangely ill and his committee's investigation of the foundations was shut down. But Carroll Reece courageously issued a statement that revealed the tremendous pressure put on him to force the closing of the investigation, on August 2, 1954, partly reading as follows:

> ". . . it seems to have become an affront for a Congressional committee to dare to subject foundations to criticism. Perhaps Congress should admit that the foundations have become . . . more powerful than the legislative branch of the Government."

The COUNCIL ON FOREIGN RELATIONS, is the key Rockefeller agency dedicated to the program that holds in its membership the top agents and key Rockefeller puppets in the United States and the UN, including: Alger Hiss, Lauchlin Currie, Frederick Vanderbilt Field, Joseph E. Johnson (who was Alger Hiss's assistant in the State Department, who was permitted to resign when a leak of top secret information to the Soviets and the enemy was traced to him, and who has fallen heir to all of Alger Hiss's key posts after he went to penetentiary), Owen Lattimore (whose indictment for perjury in connection with treasonous activities has been blocked by a Federal judge closely identified with the situation), Supreme Court Justice Felix Frankfurter (the "fall guy" and "front runner" for the conspiracy) David Dubinsky (the "organizer of the peasants") — together with the Rockefeller brothers, Nelson, David and John D III.

The Council On Foreign Relations holds the top echelon of the conspiracy. It interlocks the directorates of all of the key agencies and foundations. It openly boasts in its reports that it controls the U. S., the UN and the world; and that it manufactures "public opinion" and indoctrinates or "trains" men for government service.

The COUNCIL ON FOREIGN RELATIONS boasts in its 1952-3 annual report that, with its subsidiary "Foreign Relations Committees" (that dot the country), it has planted in the Federal Government the following top policy-making officials:

Secretary of Defense Wilson
Postmaster General Summerfield
Director for Mutual Security Stassen
Director of Budget Dodge
Adm. Assistant to President, Adams
Under Secretary of Commerce
Assistant Secretary of Defense
Assistant Secretary of State
Adviser to National Security Council
And many others.

The report discreetly refrains from mentioning that from the membership of the COUNCIL ON FOREIGN RELATIONS, whom Rockefellers designate as their chief agents, the following top flight members of our government were chosen:

PRESIDENT DWIGHT DAVID EISENHOWER
as well as his adversary Adlai Stevenson

SECRETARY OF STATE JOHN FOSTER DULLES
kinsman of the Rockefellers and their top agent.
His predecessors, including Dean Acheson, who was his subordinate, were also members.

ASSISTANT SECRETARY OF HEALTH & WELFARE NELSON ROCKEFELLER
who is the real President of the U. S.

Among the endless array of Rockefeller kinsmen and agents who constitute our governments, in this as in other administrations, there is the prize of defective pawns,

SECRETARY FOR THE ARMY
ROBERT TENBROEK STEVENS
Trustee of the Rockefeller Foundation, who despite his mentality, did cover up the fact that he was merely a pawn of the Rockefellers in bringing his charges against Sen. Joseph McCarthy

Despite the overwhelming power exercised by its members the Council on Foreign Relations has been so well shielded by the Rockefeller control of the press that it is absolutely unknown to the bulk of the nation, and the world, whose destinies are controlled by the Rockefellers through it. It is treated by the press (with the sole exception of the Chicago Tribune) as sacrosanct. It is the ideal front for the "One World" international dictatorship conspiracy.

The fidelity with which the conspirators follow the teachings of Weishaupt is portrayed by the venomous, relentless and vindictive manner in which they spy on, harass, persecute and destroy any man who dares expose their conspiracy and agents. This activity, the Rockefellers, through their "Philanthropic" Foundation Trust and its subsidiary agencies, openly finance and support. Thus in its Review For 1948 the Rockefeller Foundation published on page 64 its granting of $110,000 to Cornell University for a "Study of the relation of civil rights to the control of subversive activities in the United States." Expressed simply, the purpose of the appropriation was to harass investigators of un-American activities. A Red sympathizer, Professor Gellhorn, of Columbia University, was placed in charge of the "study."

No investigator of the un-American activities of the conspirators in Congress has escaped the Ogpu-Gestapo type of vengeance of the conspirators. It was symbolized by Weishaupt in the "all-spying eye", guarding the pyramid that represented their conspiracy and that they made the Great Seal of the U.S.A. Hamilton Fish, Martin Dies, and his attorney, Robert Stribling, J. Parnell Thomas, and Joseph McCarthy and his entire staff, Eugene Cox and Carroll Reece, have been harassed or destroyed by them.

The strange case of Senator Joseph McCarthy illustrates the methods of the conspirators. McCarthy ran for office with their support, posing as an "internationalist" of their breed. Once elected, he struck out as a "patriot." This, in the views of Weishaupt and his followers, is the most reprehensible and despicable of all offenses. Though McCarthy did not expose their sponsors and financeers, or breathe the name of Rockefeller, he repeated attacks on their traitorous agents. The Weishaupt Gestapo required relentless and concerted persecution of the "betrayer."

In 1953, President Eisenhower voiced the dictate of the conspirators that their Communist dictatorship conspiracy would not be an election issue. In August, 1953, the Nelson Rockefeller entourage openly boasted that they had McCarthy "framed" and would destroy him. Within several months, their agents made good their boast by preferring absurd charges against Sen. McCarthy and his aids, that effectively paralyzed his committee and stopped his investigation of the conspirators.

The charges filed against McCarthy and his aids by Robert Tenbroek Stevens, Trustee of the Rockefeller Foundation and puppet Secretary for the Army were primarily that he and his counsel, Roy Cohn, sought preferment in the Armed services, for one of their volunteer investigators of Communist espionage activities, David Schine. It is quite obvious that unless the Armed services were infested with Communists, they would be the first to require preferment or exemption for a man engaged in exposing spies and traitors. Such preferential treatment serves the interest of the nation and its defense rather than that of the individual involved. Such investigators expose themselves to the special fury of the enemies of the nation and its defenses; and those who attack them and seek to destroy their effectiveness, expose themselves as enemies of the nation. In the case of Schine, it is the puppet Secretary of the Army Stevens, his Rockefeller masters and their agents in and out of the government, in alliance with the entire horde of conspirators and pawns, who have exposed themselves as the enemies and betrayers of national interests. They have unanmously risen to the defense of exposed, notorious traitors in and out of the Armed Services, and done their best to destroy patriots who seek to protect the country from treason.

The Army traitors who promoted Major Peress and protected the Communist spies at Monmouth have been promoted by their traitorous superiors in the Army. McCarthy, chairman of the investigating committee, Roy Cohn, its counsel, David Schine, the investigator of the conspirators, and their patriotic collaborators have been harassed and persecuted for the purpose of discrediting them and driving them out of public life. This has been done with the active participation of notorious fellow travelers and collaborators of the conspirators in the Senate such as Stuart Symington, Ralph E. Flanders (supplier for the USSR, whose brother is a loyal friend of convicted conspirator Alger Hiss) and Red CIO agent Sen. Potter. To protect the high conspirators, their associate, President Eisenhower, issued a directive that barred their exposure. Behind the scene there is the "reorganizer" of the Defense Department, (who placed its control in "civilian" hands) the overall boss, and Presidential dictator, Nelson Rockefeller.

An even broader scene of national betrayal and treason is that presented by the conspirators' execution of Weishaupt's scheme of "internationalism." The National "Security" Councils, extra-Constitutional and super-governmental devices that have been set up in the Rockefeller Foundation and then transferred to the governments, with personnel, in the U.S.A., France and other lands, have proved to be the nests that harbor top rank Communist agents and spies who systematically betray their countries to the top conspirators and to the lands that now spearhead the conspiracy — the USSR and its satellites. Simultaneously with the exposure of such traitors in the U.S.A. and in France, and in utter contempt of public reactions of horror, the fronting agency of the conspiracy another Rockefeller-Soviet creation, the UN, openly advocates loyalty to itself and treasonous betrayal of one's native land — in publicly proclaimed instructions to its workers issued in the first week of October, 1954. Among the signers of this command of treason is one of the top-rank Rockefeller agents, member of a whole series of agencies set up in the Rockefeller Foundation and transferred to the Government, Arthur S. Flemming. Flemming's other top policy-making posts include: Economic Stabilization Agency, Office of Defense Mobilization, and Defense Mobilization Board — all ideal posts for an enemy agent.

In order to evade the refusal of Congress to appropriate funds for payment of exposed traitors in the U.S. delegation, American delegates established a special reserve fund for such payments, according to a release of the UN made in December, 1954.

This traitorous "internationalism" is immensely profitable to key Rockefeller interests. Thus, India is today a satellite of USSR and Soviet China, and is a Soviet in all but name. Agents of Rockefeller's Council on Foreign Relations and their Soviet espionage agency, Institute of Pacific Relations, including Owen Lattimore, Lauchlin Currie and Alger Hiss have played key roles in delivery of China, Korea and India to the Soviets. Every agency controlled by the Rockefeller interests, the "Philanthropic" Foundation Trust and especially the Ford Foundation, has been aiding in the process of "softening up" and enriching India in preparation for her open delivery to the Communists. The American taxpayer has been looted of billions of dollars for this "aid to India" in spite of the fact that Indian officials openly revile and betray the U.S.A. at every opportunity. Rockefeller henchmen, such as former U. S. Ambassador for India, Chester Bowles, Eleanor Roosevelt, (who is now under consideration by the Eisenhower Administration at the behest of the conspirators, as Ambassadress to India — America's oldest Red to the newest Soviet) and a host of others are being sent on pilgrimages to India and abet the conspiracy. Mutual "Security" Agency under its director Harold Stassen—a member of Rockefeller's Council of Foreign Relations and of the National "Security" (Betrayal) Council—is squandering billions of dollars of American taxpayers' money on so-called "aid to India," including hundreds of millions for the construction of railroads in India, and the indirect support of industry in Communist infested lands, to the exclusion of American industry. At the heart of this treason is profit to the Rockefeller interests. This is quite apparent in the virtual monopoly of oil refining and marketing that India has given the Standard Oil Company of New Jersey and other Rockefeller interests that are building huge refineries in India to help in the provision of refined oil products to Iron Curtain countries.

Another of the endless profits of "internationalist" treason, that has come to light, is that embodied in the treaty drawn up with Western Germany by Rockefeller kinsman and agent, Secretary of State John Foster Dulles. The treaty provides that Germany will be relieved of repayment of two billion dollars of the occupation costs to the American taxpayers, provided that Germany redeems the virtually worthless bonds of the Young and Dawes plans of the Weimar Republic, at full par value plus interest accrued for twenty years (which means at a price well over two thousand dollars each) held by "American" interests. The bondholders were represented, according to Senator Humphrey by John Foster Dulles's firm, Sullivan & Cromwell. This is a steal of two billion dollars from the American taxpayers, that is split by the conspirators with Germany.

The ugliest and most menacing phase of the conspiracy, that threatens an early end of our Republic, is the full development of Weishaupt's "bi-partisan" pattern. Through their control of the nominating machinery and all avenues of mass communication, the Rockefeller interests have succeeded in effectually robbing us of our franchise, as completely, and even more effectively, as in the Soviets. Almost all candidates for all offices are agents of the conspirators. The voters are given "Hobson's choice", between two or more Rockefeller Red agents of the "internationalist" conspiracy.

This is illustrated in a number of the 1954 political campaigns. In New Jersey the conspirators nominated two "internationalist" pawns of theirs as Senate candidates. The voters were confronted with the candidates as a "fait accompli," in which they could have no voice. The Democratic candidate, Rep. Charles R. Howell, was one of the leaders in the World Federalist movement, and a bitter pill for the electorate to swallow. The Republican candidate, Clifford P. Case, who like his opponent was endorsed by the ADA, one of the fronts of the conspiracy, was rejected in advance by the electorate and fought bitterly. His malodorous record was well known to his constitutents, because he had previously resigned from his seat in the House of Representatives to serve the conspirators directly as a paid employee of the subversive Ford Foundation. In short he regarded his services to the "Philanthropic" Foundation Trust, the most dangerous enemy of the American people, as more important than his services to his electorate. He resigned his post shortly before receiving the nomination. But it is quite obvious that he is the conspirator's candidate. Nelson Rockefeller personally campaigned for Case in Montclair and Milburn, on October 25, 1954. This marks the first occasion on which the Rockefellers have expressed openly their contempt for public opinion by openly supporting one of their malodorous agents.

In the "Republican" administration the real Republicans have been counted out, and have had no more voice than the real Democrats in the Democratic Party. Both parties have been taken over by the conspirators through the "bipartisan" device, to further the Weishaupt-Socialist-Communist dictatorship conspiracy. Eisenhower is frankly a puppet and agent of the Rockefellers, and an associate of their Red agents. In short, as the author predicted in a pamphlet published in 1952 prior to the election, EISENHOWER WILL GIVE US NO CHANGE. The millions of New Dealers that had been frozen into the Government in the two decades prior, as agents of the conspirators, were left in their posts, on the pretense of shunning the spoils system.

A new development on the political scene has been the widening and intensification of the hereditary transmission of public office in both high and low echelons. This tradition which has been highly developed by the Rockefellers in their own enterprises, is now transferred by them to all the governments that they control. By repeated usage, it has become a custom that has been supported by the persistent brainwashing directed by the Rockefeller and allied "educational," or propaganda, devices.

It has come to be accepted, in the past two decades, that because Franklin Delano Roosevelt was President, his son Franklin Jr. is also entitled to the same office; that because Robert F. Wagner, was a Senator who served the Rockefeller interests with absolute loyalty, his son, Robert F. Jr. is entitled to the same office, and that the oldest son of ex-President Hoover, should inherit his post after serving the Rockefeller interests, in Iran, as ably as had his father. Many other instances can be cited. This is a phase of the plan to overthrow our Constitutional form of government and substitute for it a monarchy — first elective, and then hereditary, that has been published by Rockefeller's adviser on sociology, Hoffman Nickerson in his book entitled THE AMERICAN RICH (Doubleday Doran, 1930).

The Rockefellers are acquiring by association and intermarriage, some of the odor of "divine right to rule" that has been established in moronic minds by the Roosevelt-Delano dynasty. They no doubt expect that it will stand them in good stead when they reach out to attain the status of "REX, IMPERATOR ET DEUS" which is the apparent goal of John D. Jr.

The Roosevelts are being pushed into the background slowly and carefully, for fear that it might upset the discipline of the "peasants", if they should be asked to shift to other loyalties suddenly. For the Roosevelts, posing as "liberals" and "friends" of all minorities, have been the traditional candidates of the conspirators for more than a century, especially since the days of Clinton Roosevelt. Thus so important was the Roosevelt name regarded by the ADA in luring the moronic "peasants" in the Los Angeles district, that it settled for a handsome sum the divorce action of Romelle Roosevelt, so as to leave Kiss-And-Tell James Roosevelt more time to conduct his campaign, immune from more malodorous and sensational divorce publicity.

Sock-Em- and Leave-Em Franklin D. Roosevelt Jr., who has distinguished himself chiefly by his pugnacity, bibacity, neglect of duty, slavish adherence to the conspirators' Party-Line and his readiness to serve for pay such obviously subversive un-American front organizations as the Independent Committee of Arts, Sciences and Professions, has traded heavily on the family name and the Clinton Roosevelt tradition. The Rockefeller henchmen denied him the Democratic nomination for the post of Governor of New York State, that he demanded as his "hereditary right". But for the purpose of luring the moronic and imbecilic votes of the "peasants", they farcically gave Junior, whose record as a trial lawyer is almost nil, the nomination for the post of Attorney General in the 1954 State election.

One of the most important sectors of the electorate to whom the Roosevelts are relied on by the conspirators to appeal, is the Jewish vote. Though it is true that his ancestors, Claes Martenszen van Rosenvelt (Dutch for Rosenfeld) and Jannetje Samuel both stemmed from renegade Jewish origin, Eleanor Roosevelt has made it quite clear how fundamentally anti-Semitic is the attitude of the family — something that is quite characteristic of renegades. In an article published in the December 31, 1938 issue of Liberty magazine, Eleanor Roosevelt suggested that Hitler had made a mistake in his treatment of the Jews. She suggested that Hitler's brutality would arouse the antagonism of the "compatriots" of the Jews in other lands; and this implied that she regarded Jews as aliens in their land of residence, and in the U. S. She suggested that though the Jews are dangerous, it would be far better to adopt the "numerus clausus," restricting the number of Jews permitted to enter any vocation; and to force the migration of Jews so that their vote would not preponderate in any section of the land. The Roosevelt progeny have never disavowed the views of their mother on the "Jewish Question".

There is a ray of hope for the nation in the fact that in the past decade the leadership of the conspiracy has deteriorated to the point that it is becoming obvious. The dictatorship of the Rockefeller Empire has been taken over, in the political field, by Nelson Rockefeller. Nelson is fond of strutting and is the first of the Rockefellers to emerge openly on the political scene. His mental attitude is quite obvious in his favorite photograph of himself—a pose, in which he was photographed by photographer Karsch, of Ottawa. It depicts him as holding the globe in his grasp. (A request made of Karsch's representatives in the U.S., the Pix agency, for use of this photo for reproduction here, was denied after cautious inquiry and investigation of the use to which it would be put.) Nelson R. presents copies of it to his friends and agents; and presented one to "Ike" Eisenhower for his desk.

For the first time during the 1954 "off year" elections, the American people became acutely aware that they have been effectively robbed of their franchise by conspirators who have taken over control of all parties and dictate the nomination of their agents as candidates. This gives the voters "Hobsons' choice" between puppets of the conspirators who are pledged to betray the nation. This is well illustrated by the candidacies of Case and Howell in New Jersey, and of Ives and Harriman in New York.

For the first time the public realized widely that they were trapped by a conspiracy and dictatorship that robs them of the right to choose their own public servants. They were confused, bewildered and only semi-articulate in their protests. Their initial reaction was to refuse to go to the polls. But puppet President Eisenhower was used to stampede them into voting by radio and television appeals, as well as by the moronic device of telephonic personal appeals to voters, chosen at random, to make chain calls to ten more voters a piece. This resulted in many more voters going to the polls than had originally intended,—with unexpected results. For a large proportion of the voters went to the polls and exercised their futile powers of protest by voting not *"for"* but *"against"* the candidates dictated by the conspirators for their respective parties. But they were as effectively robbed of any real choice as is the Soviet voter with a single candidate on his ballot. Their only choice was *Rockefeller*, via one agent or another. The result was much to the liking of the astute and cynical "planners"—the shifting of control to the Democratic agents, with whom Nelson Rockefeller has worked longer, feels more a home and trusts more. An exception was the Rockefeller Red agent Clifford Case, for whom Nelson Rockefeller came out into the open and campaigned. But even in that instance it is doubtful that in an honest vote and count, Case would have emerged victorious.

The confusion of the public is intensified by the multitude of "fronts" set up by the conspirators as devices for deluding and diverting the "peasants". These fronts pose as "anti-Communist". Thus Columbia University, one of the conspirators' key brainwashing agencies, adopted for its second centennial celebration the theme of "The Right To Knowledge"—which it so effectively suppresses. Key conspirators and their dupes, from all parts of the world, were invited to dilate upon this ironic theme for "peasant diversion'.

Another such front is "Aware Inc.", an agency that pretends to fight Communism in the field of entertainment. It has been set up by advertising executives for de-skunking their Red tinged "talent" of the stigma placed upon them by exposure in such vehicles as "Counter-Attack"; and to provide for them a "non-Communist" seal of approval that will protect their commercial value. The only "anti-Communist" expressions that the organization permits to its invited guess are restricted to the approved "anti-Communist" Party line of the conspirators, in the pattern prescribed by Weishaupt and his successors. And its "anti-Communist" speakers are largely restricted to alleged ex-Communists who carefully avert violating the approved "anti-Communist" Party line. Anyone who risks truly anti-Communist expressions at the illicitly liquor-vending meetings of the organization to which he might be invited, risks being mugged and brutally assaulted by a crew of thugs—as was the author at its October, 1954 meeting.

A spark of hope was kindled in the breasts of some naive patriots by the election of Senator Thurmond by a write-in vote. However they are doomed to disappointment. The conspirators, through the agency of the "Philanthropic" Foundation Trust, that is led by the Rockefeller foundations and dominated by them, has devoted many hundreds of millions of dollars to robbing the people of any voice in their government. They have set up a swarm of agencies, which are added to every year. The dominant agencies are the Institute of Public Administration, located next door to the building given the UN Soviet delegation as a residence for Vishinsky, Gromyko, Malik and Zarubin at the corner of 68th Street and Park Avenue, in New York City; and the Public Administration Clearing House that is known by its street address, "1313", that was provided by Rockefeller funds to house an endless array of agencies for control of local governments here and abroad. These agencies include the original of the National Resources Planning Board and the Office of Government Reports that were labelled by Congressman John Taber as *"a menace to the welfare of the American people, and . . . a menace to Constitutional government."* These Rockefeller-financed agencies include the Conferences of Governors, the Conferences of Mayors, the Conferences of District Attorneys, and a host of others that are designed to bring direct pressure to bear on public officers and to control legislation as the conspirators wish it controlled. The type of voting machines foisted on the nation by the conspirators are designed to accomplish three purposes; first, they make it impossible for the voter to know for whom his vote is recorded; second, they make "fixing" the machines and stealing elections a simple matter; and third, they make a write-in vote impossible.

These agencies, severally and collectively, have done a nefarious job of transferring the control of government to the conspirators. They have introduced such devices as Five Year Plans, that are so characteristic of the activities of the conspirators; revision of charters and Constitutions of local governments every ten years, when changes are made that more completely serve the conspirators and frustrate the public; and the setting up of legal provisions that make nomination of candidates by the public and the setting up of new, or third parties, or of effective write-in protest votes, virtually impossible in important sections of the country. The conspirators have not gotten around to perverting the government of the Carolinas to their purposes. But that oversight will not be permitted to stand long.

As we go to press, Nelson Rockefeller emerged into public eye as Presidential "Edgar Bergen." Nelson R. assumed the post of "adviser" to the President on foreign affairs, the "cold" war. Simultaneously, kinsman Joseph M. Dodge was appointed "foreign aid economic planner".

It is obvious that it is planned that Nelson Rockefeller will, at the right time, take over from his cousin John Foster Dulles the post of Secretary of State. Under the new law on Presidential succession pushed through the last Congress by the conspirators, he will then be fourth in line of succession, and only three heartbeats removed from the White House. He can then attain his Presidential ambition without the nation ever having a choice or voice in the matter.

Directly after Rockefeller's appointment, puppet "Ike" announced that the "cold" war would be extended from twenty to fifty years, so as to allow of an adequate buildup for a "hot" war with Russia. Simultaneously, it was announced by Secretary of Agriculture Benson that Russia would be aided in her buildup for the same "hot" war by the "sale", which is double-talk for "gift", to the Soviets of butter, at the expense of U.S. taxpayers. War and its preparation have been profitable to the Rockefeller interests and foundations.

While Nelson Rockefeller moves brashly in openly taking over national control, there is fear among the conspirators of public reaction and revolt. The persecution of all enemies of the conspirators is to be steadily intensified. Government agencies are being used increasingly for this task. The author on December 17, 1954 was questioned by FBI Agents Sheridan and Buhr, and by other Federal agencies in connection with his fight on Nelson's protege, Clifford Case. The FBI investigated a supposed violation of section 612 of the Election Law.

John D. Rockefeller Jr.'s "gift" of $20,000,000 for the purpose "of advancing Protestant theology" to his dummy, tax-dodging foundation, the Sealantic Fund was announced in January, 1955. Previously a gift of one million to Harvard for a school of divinity had been announced. This demonstrates the uses of "philanthropy" in the best tradition of Adam Weishaupt for the purpose of bribing public opinion. It follows a set pattern of Rockefeller "philanthropies" adopted on the advice of John D.'s in-law Rev. Dr. A. H. Strong, who wrote him:

> "Your present gifts, to education and to the churches, do not stem the tide of aspersions as would the establishment of an institution for the public good, so great that it has manifestly cost a large self-sacrifice to build it."

Whenever under attack, the Rockefellers make such "philanthropic" gesture, particularly to religion. In the early part of this century following the outraged outcry of the nation at the brutal Colorado Fuel & Iron massacre of their workers, they set up the Laura Spelman Rockefeller Memorial. It initially was entirely devoted to "charity" and support of churches; but as soon as public attention was diverted, its moneys went to the support of subversion and the Illuminist-Communist conspiracy under the direction of Beardsley Ruml. They also launched Billy Sunday on his evangelical revivalism in that era as they are now doing with Billy Graham. Weishaupt taught his followers well the value of using "religion" and "philanthropy" as a cover for the conspiracy. Rockefeller's chief Protestant philanthropy, run by kinsman John Foster Dulles, the Federal Council of Churches of Christ, was pronounced by Naval intelligence, in 1936, to be one of the most dangerous subversive institutions in the country.

These "gifts" of funds withheld from the Treasury are obviously designed to counter the exposure of the Carroll Reece Committee, a crude attempt to buy off public opinion, with the public's own funds.

Now that the public shows signs of being aroused to their betrayal, what can they do to recover control of their government from the conspirators? The new laws on treason, which were introduced by the conspirators themselves in what they thought would be an idle gesture to allay public reaction to the Communist exposures, can serve in good stead. They should be stiffened to confiscate the property of conspirators and traitors, as well as to deprive them of all civil rights including citizenship.

More important still, however, it is necessary to outlaw all privately established and controlled foundations, and to transfer all their laudable functions, if any, to the government itself. There is no justification for permitting self appointed individuals to operate with tax funds that they are permitted to withhold from the Treasury.

"Internationalism" must be treated as the treason that it is. And patriotism must be restored as a respected human trait.

Finally, if we are to recover the liberty of which the conspirators have so slyly robbed us, the Constitution must be restored as the basic law of the land. In its definition of government in terms of the maximum preservation of human liberty, it is our only safeguard against the feudalism and slavery that the conspirators have gone so far in imposing on us. Their devices such as the 16th amendment and the wholely illicit capital tax, that the Treasury has imposed on the nation under its cover and in violation of the Bill of Rights, must be abolished. We must return to the Constitutional provision that the people may be taxed and drafted *only for the defense of American territory.*

Never has our country been in greater danger—a danger that stems almost entirely from traitors from within, who have taken over control of our Government for the purpose of destroying it and enslaving us. They must be vigorously exposed and driven out, if we are to survive as a nation.

The full extent of Rockefeller "philanthropy" is revealed by an early sequel of the assumption by Nelson Rockefeller of open dictatorship of foreign policy, as so-called "adviser" to puppet "Ike". In violation of the Constitution, Congress was required to delegate its power to declare war on China; and in a second violation of the Constitution, which bars the Federal Government from engaging in any war other than waged in *defense* of the U.S.A., this threatened Chinese war is authorized for the defense of Formosa.

This war might be interpreted, incorrectly, as a continuation of the policy of the Rockefeller Empire launched in 1932. Then Henry L. Stimson, Rockefeller attorney and Secretary of State, approached President Hoover with the proposition of declaration of war on Japan, for the protection of their billions in property in invaded China, in return for assured reelection. Hoover rejected the deal because of his scruples as a Quaker. Stimson revealed that he then offered the deal to F. D. Roosevelt, who gleefully accepted. Farley related that at his first Cabinet meeting, immediately after inauguration, Roosevelt proposed declaration of war on Japan, but was dissuaded in favor of a plan to induce Japan to attack the U.S.A. This was the inception of World War II. As usual, war is Rockefeller's chief "philanthropy"; and our War Department, tagged "Defense", is headed by trustees of the Rockefeller Foundation, or their employees and associates.

However, such interpretation is erroneous. The betrayal of China to the Reds, engineered by the conspirators through the Rockefeller-financed Institute of Pacific Relations, has delivered China into their hands. The war would serve to cover up further betrayals and enable the use of American lives as decoys for further treacherous aid to the Chinese Communists. Even a war scare could serve as a pretext for the culmination of the dictatorship conspiracy at home, in the U.S.

For further information on this phase, the reader is referred to the following books by E. M. Josephson:

ROCKEFELLER "Internationalist", The Man Who Misrules The World—Chedney Press, 1952. 448 pp. $4.00

THE STRANGE DEATH OF FRANKLIN D. ROOSEVELT —Chedney Press, 1948. 333 pp. $3.00

THE

SCIENCE OF GOVERNMENT,

FOUNDED ON

NATURAL LAW.

BY

CLINTON ROOSEVELT.

NEW YORK:
PUBLISHED BY DEAN & TREVETT,
121 FULTON STREET.
1841.

PREFACE

(The author admits his superior intellect and wisdom.—Ed.)

THE last words of an author are generally given first. Prefaces are written when the books are finished. They are generally intended as explanatory of something which the work itself will not explain, and in it the author takes the liberty to introduce himself and his motives. Few people, therefore, read the Preface, and perhaps it is as well to overlook it. The present writer acknowledges he has nothing in particular to say. The work was called for by some of his friends, who heard his lectures at the City Hall some two or three winters ago, and he has written it, rather hastily perhaps, within a few days past. A larger work would have been more imposing in appearance, *but the truth is, large works and long speeches are rarely made by men of powerful thought. The giant draws up by the roots the tree, which the pigmy hacks upon the livelong day.* The little man may say it was not *done secundum antem*—not, nicely or critically. *The giant says the work is done, and points him to his prostrate enemy.* This for illustration, not to boast, but as an apology for so small a work, upon so great a subject—*the greatest, by the way, of all the sciences, as it includes all others; the most benevolent, as it is intended to bring all to bear, for the greatest good of all mankind, now, and to come on earth.*

As to boasting, the writer is well aware it is the worst policy imaginable, for any one in search of admiration. He had better seem extremely modest, make apologies, advance with cap in hand on tiptoe. This is the way to captivate all little minds, without a single spark of genius, in a work. But the object of the author is to speak exactly as he thinks, with mathematical precision. *Truth may seem severe when it is not, and he who speaks it, like the skilful surgeon at an amputation, calmly cuts, but only to save life or reputation.* The man who will not do so is a moral coward. He is unfit to speak, or write, or act. He is selfish, and a *selfish man is ready to do anything. He only fears the law, or sword, or pistol. But little mean minds look only at the present apparent good, regardless of all greater good and evil in the future.* And there must ever be a war between the dispositions of the classes who look only at the present, and only at the future. We must look at both at once. But to effect a great and good result, all things must be TRUE TO NATURE. The simplest carpenter's apprentice can tell you from experience, that if the joints of any frame work *are not true, the parts will not fit well when put together, and it will rack down, and shake to pieces, at the first storm, which may arise. But the unwise think that they are wise,* when *they are only cunning.* They know not the sublimity of simple truth, and when a man with the full consciousness that he has done a noble work, may seem to feel its dignity, they cry "behold how vain!" Not seeing the great work which does ennoble him, they think him vain even on the merest trifles. They judge of others by themselves. Still let us speak the truth if, not in works of fiction, at least when great interests are at stake. How elevated, how sublime indeed the sentiment of *Sir Henry Wotton,* on this subject.

"How happy is he born or taught
"Who serveth not another's will,
"Whose armor is his honest thought,
"And simple truth his highest skill.

"This man is freed from servile bands,
"Of hope to rise and fear to fall.
"Lord of himself if not of lands,
"And having nothing, yet hath all."

(Critics must have his prescience and unmatched wisdom—"Papa knows best."—Ed.)

To resume :—

As it cannot be expected, that a new science of government complete, and founded on a law of motives which no system of education or philosophy has recognized, can possibly escape the envenomed shafts of such, as would, but cannot show an original idea, we desire only to say one thing to arbitrators and thinkers for the public—think first of yourselves what is necessary to just criticism. If you do not know, allow us then to hint it to you. *First, a heart to feel for all the woes of all mankind, and not for those only which press now upon the senses, but for all time past, and for all time to come;* and secondly, *there must also be perception, with power like an eagle's eye, to see at a glance from far beyond the reach of vulgar organs, not merely the hare to satisfy his present want, but all the vast extent of states and empires, with one, and with the other eye, the sun which gives light to the earth.*

Learned men have long contended that it was impossible for any human intellect to grasp what has been here attempted,—that a Cyclopædia only, could embrace in one view, all the arts and sciences, which minister to man's necessity and happiness— and that they give but little credit for, as a Cyclopædia is a mere arbitrary alphabetical arrangement. We would not say we have done even what we have, without much toil and sacrifice. *It has cost the best ten years of the writer's life, to settle its great principles, and give it form and substance.* The world has been the book, the teacher, God and nature. The mere writing is most unimportant. The thought is all. The great interests of man were in a state of chaos, and this science is to harmonize them, and run side by side with *true religion,* so far as that is meant, "*to feed the hungry, clothe the naked, and make on earth, peace and good will to man.*"

These remarks are made, that none may lightly damn the work. Let them, we repeat, examine first their own hearts and heads, and learn if they are qualified to speak or write upon it. The poorest and most ignorant, with sound moral and mental powers, has faculties to judge, far better than he, who with envious and contracted feelings, seeks only to detract from good, and embitter the existence of such as they may envy, but not emulate, with all of their advantages of Greek, and Latin, Hebrew, Chaldee, and Arabic, nouns and pronouns.

This is the age of words. We mean in political and moral science, as well we fear, as in true religion. While mechanical and chemical sciences are advancing with such rapid strides, that excessive production has become a bugbear, the *vast majority of the most enlightened nations are now dying from diseases superinduced by excessive labor, and deficient nourishment, and clothing. It is all owing to vapid words, words, words. Men should be ashamed to write huge tomes, while those who want the information most, have neither time to read nor means to buy.*

There is such a thing as learned verbose folly, and also pigmies in long gowns on stilts; and they may nod or shake their heads, like plaster Chinese Mandarins, as dealers in small wares may pull the wires for effect; but the people need not care, and *to the people we appeal from all self-constituted arbiters.* But liberal criticism will be accepted as a favor; and writers who may undertake the task, will confer an obligation by directing a copy of their articles, to the author at New York, from England, France, or Germany, or any part of our own country, where this work may reach. Such as may take the trouble will receive the author's best acknowledgments. His tone may seem not strictly according to *bien science*, and he must claim indulgence from the men of real judgment and good feeling, while he lashes out the money changers from the temples of just criticism. They expect a tribute, and we pay them in advance.

THE

SCIENCE OF GOVERNMENT, FOUNDED ON NATURAL LAW.

(Author voices plaint of workers.—Ed.)

Producer. I toil, and others reap the fruits. Who will show me real good! To whatsoever point I turn my sorrowing regards, nought but misery, and the prospect of still greater misery do I witness. Whichsoever party gains the victory, WE still bear the burdens of society. In Great Britain also, the land from which our statesmen with an apparent consciousness of mental weakness, copy all their precedents and principles of law and government, it is self-evident, that with the increase of the means of happiness, the great body of producers have the less and less, and if like causes still effect like consequences, so must it be in time with us, when our public lands shall all be occupied. Yea, even now, those who produce the most by genius and industry secure the least, while those who seek not to perform that which is truly useful to society, accumulate the most of all the fruits, of toil and ingenuity.

Turn we to the law for Justice? Even when grossly and directly wronged, there is no hope for us who most require the strong arm of law and government in our behalf—not for the strong but weak, was government ostensibly created. But bands of monopolists have corrupted legislators, and if we go to law, the cause may be referred and re-referred, accumulating costs at every stage of progress, until expenses swamp us in despair. No door of justice can be opened by the humble citizen, when once he has been robbed legally by artful men, of that, of which the courts themselves desire to obtain possession—money. Cerberus guards the portals to the courts of justice, falsely so called, and he must have his legal bribe, which we, who have not, cannot give. Should we essay to plead in our own sad behalf, multitudes on multitudes of books beset our path, and we gain nought but ridicule. When rich monopolists raise prices in opposition to the spirit of the laws by their floods of paper, they go free, but when we seek to meet the most *unjust depreciation in the value of the money given us as wages, we are sent to prison as conspirators.* If we ask our highest learned *institutions* for a *better system of Political Economy, by which we may obtain the means of meeting monied power on the ground of money, we are told, "let men alone and things will regulate themselves." Then send us off, to*

"Beg a fellow worm to give us leave to toil."

And dreadful and savage is the thought! the more that we produce, the nearer are we to starvation. When the master manufacturer cannot sell as rapidly as we can make, we are discharged to pine away, until those in better circumstances can waste and wear out the excess of our productions. In *Great Britain*—the land from which our Political Economy is also borrowed—"*bastiles" have been erected, as the only means to cure the crime of poverty. A sight of the green fields is denied unhappy inmates —partners for life are parted—the poor maiden's only ornament, her glossy locks of hair, are closely cropped, as if a criminal—her wrists and neck are placed in stocks, while monsters thus despoil the destitute; and all for what? Those in better circumstances cannot consume or waste in riot, as rapidly as her poor companions and herself can produce the means of living happily, and when she asks a pittance from the poor rates, to prevent direct starvation, she thus suffers for excessive industry.*

(Author voices need of "internationalism." —Ed.)

In the mean time, want increases with the increase of the means of living happily. We become the rivals of soulless insensible machinery. We are told there are too many of us. We are forbidden to look even to affection from some tender partner, as a solace to our misery—I mean we in England, Ireland, France, and elsewhere, for our cause is one over the wide earth. *We the producers are the slaves of all governments alike.*

In England, those who know not the great difficulties of their lot, complain of corn-laws, tithes, or want of universal suffrage. Others say the great monopoly of land, is the master curse, and others say, "let all things be in common, and let there be no accountability to government."

(Monetary system is at fault.—Ed.)

We in America, have no corn laws, tithes, or hinderance to almost universal suffrage. Land, also, is almost as free as air, if we choose to settle in the great territories of the public; but natural evils then arise from isolation, sickness and death may visit us, and none to help be near. We are social beings, and we wish to live together. *If we strive to do so, we are rivals to the poor of Europe.* They undersell us in our markets, and tens of thousands of us at a time are often destitute. If our short-sighted statesmen *seek protection from a tariff, they at the same time issue paper money, and by raising the prices of the raw material, rents, interest of money, and all other things, they thus nullify their work,* and even give the foreign manufacturer an advantage over our own, and bring the nation annually in debt fifteen millions on an average, as our domestic enemies acknowledge when hard pressed, and for which our most available stocks and property are now mortgaged :—so short sighted are our elected representatives. This has been the case for years, and those who first proposed the remedy (a *reformation of the banking system,*) when the union was shaken to its centre, by the danger of a civil war between the North and South; have had exhausted on them every epithet that low imagination could devise.

(Remedy is class welfare of labor against capital "that is ordained by God"—Ed.)

Fashions which worship crosses, stars and garters, which are given to such as ravage and destroy, with fire and sword, the territories of the peaceful husbandman and civil citizen, have been brought to bear against us. The great banker, like the robber by the sword, men consider good society, while the honest man of value to his fellow men, is held as base, ignoble, vulgar, and looked down upon with scorn. Honest industry being thus despised, we are too generally led to seek to overreach by plausible pretences, rather than live by juster means; and virtue, suffering persecution, flees from earth. In despair, I ask again—Who can show me what is truly good? What seems at first view to be good, is evil in its consequences, and what at first seems evil, and is undesired, is in the end superior to that which we most ardently desired as good. Ah me! What can I and my class do? *We are beasts of burden. If I look to heaven, its ministers I find are also "laying on our shoulders burdens grievous to be borne, while they will not move a little finger" in our favor.* I turn to them and turn away, and back to them again, since they make most pretensions of good will to man, *but it is all a show.* They too are striving to escape *that hydra, want, and seek the glory of the world, and dare not speak against the great accumulator.* In view of all we thus behold, does not the dreadful thought come home to our understandings, *that there is no God of justice to order things aright on earth; if there be a God, he is a malicious and revengeful being, who created us for misery.* If so, why toil for happiness? Who, I cry again, in deep despair, can show me real good?

Author. I can.

P. Thou! art thou happy? Physician heal thyself. Dost thou want nothing?

A. Yea; I wish to make thee happy.

P. Why not first be happy of thyself, and give me an example?

A. Because, our good and great wise Creator, has connected all mankind, by the indisoluble ties of sympathy, so that none can be entirely happy or unhappy by himself alone. We must assist each other.

P. Why were we thus created?

A. Because much greater good can come from many, than from any one alone.

P. But I do not believe that God is good. What you say may be, still does not exist. If you insist, explain then to me, why are we unhappy? If it had ever been intended that we should have happiness on earth, why was it not created when the earth was made, and why was it not continued? It is folly to pretend to me, that free agency was necessary to man's accountability. *We care not for a dogma of a theory, what we want is happiness.* But as to free agency, the strongest motive, or what seems strongest to our understandings when it is not overthrown by out temperaments, rules our wills, nor did we create our temperaments. It is easier to present motives unto others, than to ourselves, and to take a city, than to conquer our own spirits, and govern our circumstances. We deserve then punishments, far more for others crimes, than for our own, for aught that I can find in true philosophy. But this excuse to punish is not the object of a benevolent Creator. Such an one desires no excuse to make us miserable, now, or in eternity. Happiness must be the aim of a good being, for his creatures; and we are exceedingly unhappy. I look not at the means, but at results, and if free-agency—a term which contradicts itself—must be thrown in the way of our happiness, it only proves our happiness was of small importance in the mind of our Creator, and restores my first position. God is not benevolent, and never intended us for happiness, and it is folly to exert ourselves, excepting to overreach and cheat, and then become a saint when we are rich. Such men gain the honors and glories of the world, and must be approved of God, whom they consider as selfish, and caring only for his own low glory; and they say if God, for his glory, sacrifices any creature's happiness, why may not they also? They think men wise or foolish just as they are less or more benevolent, and the more they sacrifice for others' good, the greater is their folly, and the less they sacrifice and richer they become, the greater is their wisdom. *Theories of system-makers are all visionary. Take care of yourself, they say, and your friends will value you more highly, than if you were to save the world from degradation or starvation.* The wisdom I now teach you is the practical —yours the theoretical. My only wish for my own part is, that I may have the opportunity, and whosoever else may sink or swim hereafter, I intend to float, and that without a theory of any kind whatever. I'll take the good that may drift near me of the wrecks of fortune when the law does not forbid.

As for religion, I am ready to profess the faith in which I have been educated, without scruples, regardless of all moral principles or considerations, which are only "filthy rags."

A. In other words, do you confess you mean to be a scoundrel, sir?

P. Yes, *but I do not like the term.* It is not reputable . There *is nothing like a good appearance.*

A. *Neither is the name of a producer fashionable.*

P. No; and I mean to leave it. *Besides, those who produce all, secure nothing; while those who overreach, gain all at last.* I mean to be a pious gentleman, and trade and bargain fairly, as others do; and hereafter care for myself and be respectable.

A. And when you gain your carriage, as you may if you look only to pecuniary gains regardless of all others, allow me to recommend a motto and device. Make an ass, dancing amongst young poultry, crying "every man for himself! every man for himself!" It will be homely, but it will be strong and true.

P. Well, it is not the doctrine of our colleges? What do they teach on Political Economy but this, "let men alone and things will regulate themselves." "Each man," say the learned professors of Political Economy, "knows best his own interests, and we are all by nature more inclined to regard ourselves than others; therefore, each has only to pursue his own self-interest, and all interests will be pursued of course in the best manner possible, since there is in nature a fitness of things." That is their doctrine, but where the fitness is in practice I have never seen, whatever it may be in theory. So is the theory of Miss Wright as good as any taught as practical in our higher institutions; for it is the same in principle, and may be summed up thus: "Consult the good only of the community, and individual interests will of course be best consulted, as the community interest embraces all our lesser interests." Her opponents teach only the converse of her greatest proposition. Why then has this outcry been raised up against her. Of the two, her application of the principle is most benevolent. Is is only TOO CON-

FIDING in the justice, and virtue, and wisdom of mankind. But there is no difference in the greatest principle of Adam Smith, Say, Ricardo, Wayland, and Miss Wright (now Madame Darismond,) or Mr. Owen, on the subject of wealth of nations and communities. *As Adam Smith contended there should be no national bargains to prevent free inter-charges between nations of national advantages, so Miss Wright and Mr. Owen contended, on precisely the same general principles, that there should be no bargains between individuals. You yourself, sir, were the first to urge this on our learned institutions, and what was their reply?*

A. None have taken up the gauntlet. Probably they have thought the proposition too startling or ridiculous even to be noticed.

P. No, that is not the reason. *Make a doctrine fashionable, and pay men well for teaching it, and however demoralizing it may be, a respectable professorship will keep men quiet.* Then, I pray you, call me not a scoundrel, if I resolve to follow the teaching and example of my "betters," as they are termed in good society.

A. My object, sir, was not, and is not, to insult you, or any man, or any class of men. I use hard words, *as surgeons and divines make use of them in their vocabularies, with no intention to abuse.* Abusive language is in print especially intolerable, excepting in the columns of political news-sheets. I pray you then return to a dispassionate inquiry.

P. With pleasure. I ask then, why, if God be good, are we unhappy; since if he be evil, it is folly to exert ourselves for good?

A. I answer: *Because it was impossible to create happiness immediately.*

P. Is not this a mere subterfuge? See in the universe the evidences of power without bounds, and wisdom inconceivable to accomplish other ends, and leave men miserable. There is nothing God cannot accomplish.

A. You mistake his powers.

P. Give me an example of a want of power.

A. *Necessity is superior to all other powers.* Two mountains for example, could not be created side by side without an intervening valley. If the mountains be made, the valley also must be made. *So if good be made, some evil must be made.* The allegory of the tree of knowledge is strictly philosophical.

P. Prove your positions.

A. God could not make a self-existent being, as the idea is absurd. He could not therefore make a being with *self-existent knowledge,* since there must be a *commencement to created wisdom.* Simple sensation not being wisdom, and *wisdom being the result of comparisons of opposite sensations, of which mere words could give us no idea without experience of their meaning;* it is thus only, that we may avoid the evil and choose the good, and be happy in the escape from one, and possession of the other.

P. May we not feel pleasure and pain from sympathy?

A. Yes; but that alters not the truth of the argument.

P. Subjection to pain, then, is not an evil, by your philosophy?

A. *No.* It was necessary to guard us, and prevent a retrograde movement to that state, out of which the supreme intelligence desired to elevate us. I mean death and disorganization, chaos.

P. What then is evil?

A. The *chaos of ancient night, is the great evil; and all misery arises only from what* tends to reduce man and nature to that state, in opposition to the laws of the supreme intelligence—God.

P. What is good?

A. All of the perfect organizations created from chaos, by the supreme intelligence.

P. Why are they good?

A. Because, the more perfect the organization of any created intelligent being, the more happiness may he enjoy, and the more perfect the organization of the means of happiness, the more happiness may he procure. Hence, all the wisdom of man may be concentrated in two sentences.

P. What are those profound deductions?

A. 1st. ORGANIZE ACCORDING TO THE LAWS OF THE GOD OF NATURE.

2nd. DISORGANIZE NOT, UNLESS TO CREATE SUPERIOR ORGANIZATIONS.

P. Is there any original evil, and if so, whence did it arise?

(Religion is false.—Ed.)

A. Original evil is self-existent, as darkness prevails instantly on the withdrawal of light. Cold exists where there is no heat. Death, where there is no life. Silence, where there is no sound, and chaos, where order has not been established by superior power and intelligence. Ignorance and indolence exist also of themselves, where wisdom has not been acquired, or industrious habits formed. Thus, false ideas of God and man, and the interests of society, prevail, and misery is the consequence. Of course the wiser men become, the better can they read the reason of the laws of nature's God, and the higher the ideas they then form of Deity.

P. Prove this by examples.

A. In barbarous ages they have cruel and bloodthirsty Gods, and as men become more civilized, they blush at the religions of their ancestors. We may know the degree of civilization of an age, or a sect, or individuals, by the character of the Gods they worship. Fear is the natural punishment of blasphemy, and love, the reward of justice to the character and disposition of our adorable and benevolent Creator.

P. Why then does not revelation teach the same to all.

A. Men read the bible as they do the book of nature. Each one lays a stress on certain laws, or texts, and lightly passes over others, and thus creeds as contradictory as all the systems of philosophy prevail, and contending christians have too often burnt, and scourged, and crucified their brethren, each fancying he did God service and his victim also, when he sought to save his soul from hell by a temporary severity, which was as nothing to eternal torment. *Under the garb of christianity—intended for man's greatest good—ignorance and bigotry, have filled the world with blood.*

P. Do you then oppose religion also?

A. Not by any means; I desire to "feed the hungry, and clothe the naked, to make peace on earth, and good will amongst men." All sects are useful in their times and places. Even the horrors of every kind of superstitions, are a spur to rouse the torpid savage to look up and discover the true God, and love and venerate perfection.

P. Why then seek out new principles of government?

("Natural law" only, is true."—Ed.)

A. Because there is much misery, as you acknowledge, and although "whatever is is right" amongst ideas in our minds, there is existing a desire to improve, and in things a fitness for improvement, and higher and higher happiness, just in proportion to the degree to which we exercise in the right way our faith, industry and genius. It is right to follow nature humbly.

P. What general proof have you, in natural law, of the good intentions of the Deity in our creation.

A. There is no organization to perpetuate pain in any sensitive being; on the contrary, there is a natural tendency to health when injured, and every being may be the happier the better he is organized; and when the means of happiness are lost, or by any accident the system is so far disorganized, that there is no chance for health and more pleasure than pain from existence, death is sent as a relief from anguish. In momentary agony fainting follows, and creates insensibility to pain.

P. But men fear death, even when in misery.

A. This is a wise provision, to prevent us from throwing off our lives on any transient ill, or slight disgust. In all cases where we most imagine evil, in our ignorance, there do we discover good, when wise enough to understand the great design of our almighty, all-wise and infinitely good Creator.

P. Being for the present satisfied as to your views of the great designs of Providence, I now anxiously inquire, on what principles are human governments to be constructed?

A. I have answered in general terms—we must organize according to natural laws.

P. How will you commence?

A. We must look on man as he is, and not as our prejudices lead us to believe he should be; and we must adapt *our system to him as we find him, making it an instrument in his hands for continuous improvements.*

P. Is this possible, amidst all the variety of men and things and clashing interests in society?

A. I grant society is in a state of chaos—the hand of every man is raised against his neighbor, in a low, cunning, selfish, overreaching competition, in which the strong is snatching from the weak his bread, and when he has enough, he still cries more, more, and is not satisfied. I grant that men reputed wise, and exercising at their ease their conscious strength, teach as the only true philosophy, "*laissez nous faire*—Let us alone." I know that those who most require help, are as it were on a lee-coast, and in a leaky ship, and must toil night and day to save themselves from sinking, and that those who might give them their assistance, are thinking only of themselves, by *the false philosophy of wealth,* and *of our colleges and universities.* But still I hope. There is sympathy and benevolence, as well as selfishness, in man. I appeal to both benevolence and selfishness, as both exist in man.

P. As they are opposing principles, how can you appeal to both at once?

(Regimentation is only solution.—Ed.)

A. The grand principle herein advocated is, to HARMONIZE THE INTERESTS OF MEN BY AN ORGANIZATION OF MEN AND THINGS, BY WHICH IT WILL BE TO THE IMMEDIATE SELF-INTEREST OF EVERY ONE TO ACT CONSISTENTLY WITH THE GREATEST GOOD OF ALL.

P. Do you desire to effect a common stock system?

A. Not by any means.

P. How, on your principle, can you do otherwise?

A. Take an example from a regular army. Every blow a soldier strikes, and every shot he fires, is as much to the advantage of every other soldier of the army of which he is a member, as to his own gain. In the mean time, he has his own private pay and share of spoils to use as he desires, so that there is an union in action, and mutual assistance, without an amalgamation of self-interests. This I believe to be the great desideratum, and with the gratification of the desire for immediate returns for good endeavors, and immediate accountability for evil deeds, the system must be perfect.

P. But so many systems have been tried, and now so many are proposed, how can you promise more success than others which have gone before?

A. We have all of their experience to warn us of the breakers, and every shipwreck is a beacon to succeeding mariners.

P. But no outward physical arrangements can reform society. The heart must be the seat of reformation.

A. *We have no objections to the reformation of bad hearts; far the contrary; but a pirate in a new and well found ship at sea, with a good understanding of the art of navigation, will weather many a storm in which pilgrims and missionaries in an old leaky vessel would be sure to perish.* We desire to get a system useful alike to all, to prevent necessity for crime and extreme misery. All may profit by it, for each law of nature has its own penalty, and own reward. The laws of nature are the laws of nature's God. *The book of nature is God's oldest book, and therefore should be studied first. On this we base our system.*

P. What great lessons have you learned from it?

A. We have mentioned some, and now we give another, which will show the reason why all systems of government, heretofore tried, have failed to be perpetual, and render mankind happy.

P. Can you trace the destruction of all forms of government to one simple source, when historians and statesmen give so many reasons for the decline and fall of Empires and Republics?

A. Yes. All can be traced back to a law of motives, which governs all human wills to greater or less degrees in different individuals.

P. What law of motives do you thus refer to?

A. IT IS A LAW ANALOGOUS TO THE GREAT LAW OF ATTRACTION, BY WHICH A SMALL OBJECT WHICH IS NEAR, HAS A GREATER INFLUENCE OVER THE WILL,

THAN THE GREATEST WHOSE CONSEQUENCES ARE REMOTE.

P. How do you prove the existence of such a law of motives.

A. There are many men who thoroughly believe in future rewards and punishments, but who still give way to present trifling temptations, and do not begin to fear until death approaches and awakens all their terrors. There are none who have the right to say they are above this law.

P. How does the operation of this law overthrow all governments, and even the religion of too many minds?

A. Because, in the present deficiency of organization in society, the immediate interests of men are adverse to the general good; which therefore is neglected by the well-disposed, and preyed on by the selfish, and those not selfish, but under the pressure of necessity.

P. I desire to hear examples.

A. It is to the immediate self-interest of lawyers to sustain a veneration for old abuses, even if they be "flatly absurd and unjust," and they do so, and oppose most pertinaciously every effort to introduce an amicable and cheap system of arbitrations, on equitable principles.* Hence all the expenses of the courts, the technicalities and forms of law, and uncertainties and delays of justice.

It is to the immediate self-interest of physicians to palliate diseases, rather than eradicate them; to be plausible and popular, rather than profound. To prevent diseases entirely, would be to destroy their means of living.

It is to the immediate self-interest of merchants to export from Ireland, beef, butter, potatoes and manufactures, while the people are starving and naked, to this country, where we have all the natural advantages of producing and manufacturing, —to bring the people in debt many millions annually by excessive imports, because they gain a private pecuniary profit by so doing.

*See Blackstone's Commentaries, by Chitty, page 47, Eighteenth London Edition, where it is plainly acknowledged, that "precedents and rules should be followed if flatly absurd and unjust if agreeable to ancient principles."

It is to the direct self-interest of bankers to expand and contract the currency, in order to raise and depress prices, and force men to sacrifice to them, through brokers, sheriffs and auctioneers.

It is to the direct self-interest of editors to bepraise those who will fee them best, and belie the men of honor, who despise their selfish and contracted policy.

It is to the direct self-interest of publishers to print the most frivolous and demoralizing romances, rather than the most profound works of philosophy, religion and the useful sciences.

It is to the immediate self-interest of workingmen to destroy machinery which comes in competition with their means of living.

It is to the immediate self-interest of all to rob inventors.

It is to the immediate self-interest of soldiers to have war, thus to obtain bloody spoils.

Thus we find that when men would do good, evil is necessary to support existence, and many a noble spirit mourns that he cannot give exercise to his highest aspirations for the good of all, without the sacrifice of himself and family upon the altar of his patriotism. This condition is unnatural to men of noble, sympathetic minds.

(All existent governments are corrupt shams. —Ed.)

P. Why do not legislators—the people's representatives—strive to effect a reformation by legal measures? In other words, what is there wrong in our republican system of government, that it has not effected the greatest good?

A. Our system of government is perhaps the best which could have been adopted under the circumstances. It is a system of compromise based upon the British model, and our laws are also founded on Anglo-Roman principles and precedents.

In outward form, the Houses of Assembly are copied from the House of Commons, and the Senates from the House of Lords. The first are elected for the shorter terms, the last for longer. The President is in the place of the Sovereign.

But the outward forms of government are not of

much importance. They are used as masqueraders use their dresses—to disguise their persons. There is a power behind the throne, and greater than the throne, which says to King and Parliament you shall or shall not go to war. You shall sustain the laws and constitution, or you shall suspend them both at our option. Which taxes as it pleases, and that without responsibility to any but stockholders. The reader can too easily divine the nature of this power, for it is now grinding America as well as England in the dust. It is the banking system and its leader in this country has acknowledged, that by it alone, he and his class had the power to "make men willing to make sacrifices."* It is done simply by lending and withdrawing at certain times and places, and taking advantage of scarcities of money artfully created to buy at sacrifices *and also to gain usury.*

Blackstone truly has observed, that the outward form of government is of no importance. The government is in the real rulers who cause the laws to be enacted, and suspended as may best suit their own convenience. Again :—

It is to the immediate self-interest of nominating committee-men, to sell their votes to demagogues without principles, and for demagogues in Legislatures to sell their votes to their best patrons, and make fraudulent grants of monopolies, especial privileges, and suspension acts. There is *prima facie* as well as other evidence that all this has been done, and only the theory of a republic now remains existent.

Thus in England also, when a man has moral influence, he is bought over by a place or pension, if to crush him would be dangerous. If very great, he then is made a peer, and all his opposition ceases. It is immediate self-interest from first to last, in every form of government alike. Even the greatest

---

*Biddle's letter published in Gouge's History of Banking. "The operation proceeds thus. By issuing no new notes but requiring something from your debtors, you oblige them to return to you the bank notes you lent them on their equivalents. This makes bank notes scarcer—this makes them more valuable—this makes the goods which they are generally exchanged for less valuable—the debtor in his anxiety to get your notes being WILLING TO SELL HIS GOODS AT A SACRIFICE."—First Edition, Page 191.

emperors are generally ruled by favorites, and are strangers to their people. When they operate against the immediate self-interest of courtiers, even the greatest have reason to tremble for their crowns or heads.

All governments are thus alike, and the only real difference of importance is in the administration of them. "That which is best administered is best." They are variable, and dependent on the master spirit who raises up himself above the law, and looks upon his sovereign as his instrument—a "cerimony," or mere puppet in his hands. Sometimes it is true, the sovereign has the master mind, but it is not the case in general. *In all countries, enquire who it is who can command the greatest funds and property, and there you will find the government.* The outward pageantry is used merely to amuse the vulgar, *who look only at externals*—music, songs, banners, carriages. Editors, coachmen, legislators, judges, and counsellors at law, alike with few exceptions, all quiet their consciences in the mean time, on the plea of absolute necessity and say:

> "You take my house, when you do take the prop
> That doth sustain my house; you take my life,
> When you do take the means whereby I live,"

and I submit. Shipmates starving on a raft at sea, will devour each other from necessity, and mother's drink their offspring's blood when pressed by absolute necessity. *It is necessity operating on the means of living, which now rules the world.* Those of us not under that iron crown, have reason to bless God, not that we are not like other men, but have not been as sorely tried. Some will die for honor, and nearly all would doubtless act according to the noblest principles, had they the opportunity. *Unite the interests of men and they unite—divide their interests and they arrange themselves against each other in the deadly combat.* All this may seem too clear to be repeated, and yet men too generally overlook this simple axiom in their *pretending sciences of law and government,* political economy, social systems and principles of education. *In all these cases men imagine abstract reasoning on morals and religion will have influence. They may restrain to some degree, but the master feeling conquers in the end. Self-preservation overcomes all weaker influences.*

P. What think you of Robert Owen's system?

A. I have answered it already by the principle laid down. It is to the immediate self-interest of the indolent not to labor, and it is to the like interest of industrious and acquisitive not to labor for the idle. Besides, there is no accountability. It is supposed that reasoning on abstract principles will be sufficient to overcome inertia in the idle, and create forbearance in the active and impatient. At the same time it is contended, that men are plastic, and can only be what they are taught to be by their progenitors and circumstances. Then if our *fathers were not wise, must ignorance go round and round in eternal circle?* It is said they were not. There is then no hope for man; for who can teach us any good, if we can look for wisdom only to our ignorant progenitors and circumstances, which now make misery as much as ever.

P. What think you of the system of M. Fourier?

A. I think it an abstraction. I do not think it practical for all. It professes to be based upon analogies but it is not strictly analogical. There is much in it that is good as well as in Mr. Owen's, but the work wants wheels to many of its "pivots," and it also wants a motive power. As in the case of Mr. Owen's system, there is no repulsive power, no accountability. If man's spirit be as if magnetic and subject to attractive industry, there must be something to repel from natural inertia. *We are as well fitted by nature to be repelled by what we have reason to fear, as attracted by what we hope for.* There must be laws and prisons, or hospitals, for men not sane enough to act on honest principles. What if men prove so selfish as to refuse to be attracted? In that case we apprehend that all the world would be in hospitals for monomania :—only M. Fourier and his followers would be at large. It has long ago been said that were all men philosophers, or good christians, all government would be unnecessary. It is because men have a selfish principle in them, that government is necessary. The only reason why the robber plunders and murders is, because he cares not how much others may suffer if he only may enjoy. Moreover, there is a law of Providence which says, that what man does not value sufficiently to guard as well as gain, that shall he not continue to enjoy. Every animal has offensive or defensive means appointed him by Providence. The bee has his sting to guard his sweets, the bull has horns, the horse can kick and bite and drive invaders from his pastures. According to analogy, man cannot, with safety, make an exception of himself, while any have passions.

P. But the shakers live without arms or laws.

A. Yes, but our government protects them, and a statesman never trusts to the protection of a foreign power. The wise man looks within for his resources, and in time of peace prepares for war. None can tell how long even the government we have—which is better far than none—is destined to endure. Anarchy must come at length, unless a reformation should be previously produced. Then, where would be a system without offensive or defensive means?

But M. Fourier says—or his interpreter speaks for him thus—"It is the great error of philosophers, politicians and framers of systems, in devising social institutions, to wish to suit them to man as they find him."

To many it must seem as absurd to make a system perfect in the abstract, for an imperfect being, as to make—to use a familiar illustration—a boot, fit only for a perfect foot, for an individual whose foot was crumped. He could not draw it on, and the more perfect in itself considered it might be, the more useless for him, would it be sure to be. An iron shoe which might compress and turn the foot around, to its more natural position, would be far more scientific in the end.

And it is thus men do arise from barbarism. *First, the law of force, the conqueror's arms, are necessary; next come arbitrary laws, and justice by science is slow to follow on at last.* The rude cannot appreciate the wise or good, until they know by sad experience the evils of misgovernment, or the constraint improper distortions of the mind may render necessary. The brutal should be used as brutes or or slaves. He who can consent to toil without a thought of rising to intellectual superiority, deserves to be slave, and such are rendered so. God is just in all his dispensations. But again :—M. Fourier does not recognize phrenology as true, and his arrangement of the passions seems to me to be arbitrary. In the mean time liberal phrenology is gaining more and more testimony in its favor, from the learned. If phrenology be true, the passional system advocated by M. Fourier is without foundation, and if that system be false, all founded on it is so likewise. According to the laws of nature, individual perfections is as undesirable as it is unattainable. General perfection comes from the fitness of parts. The harmony of society should be effected on the same principle that the leader of an orchestra arranges all the voices in a choir—each individual to perform the part to which his voice is by nature best adapted, each supplying the deficiency of others having other parts, and thus effecting harmony from an union and interchange of excellences. As the sculptor who desired to make a perfect statue sought through Greece for individual excellencies to unite them all in one, so *should the philanthropist seek to make one great and perfect mind of all the individuals in society. Individual perfection, excepting as a member of society, seems to be out of the nature of things.* There is much wisdom in the homely proverb that "a Jack at all trades can be good at none." Groups of organs give to every mind some peculiar excellence, while almost every one has some deficiency, which it is to his interest to have supplied by friends, or by society, arranged in *such an order as to sustain each other, and not take advantages of our individual weaknesses.* With such a system, individual excellences and defects will tend to draw society together in a closer bond of union, from self-interest; and thus may universal sympathy and love grow out of the union and prevail by scientific means. *We find in armies, even where the business is to butcher our fellow creatures, an Esprit du*

Corps arises from the mutual dependence which all feel in action: and thus, according to the ways of Providence, good arises out of evil. Out of the selfish principle, united to destroy, a spirit of love and harmony is mysteriously engendered, *by the true co-operation.*

P. Why will not the present banking system of government which has taken the place to a great extent, and continues to spread over other governments, have also a like effect?

A. Because there is no great union or mutual interest consulted. It operates against the interests of people, as *well as all established governments, until it rules kings as well as people absolutely. The law of force is not worse than the law of fraud and corruption, which is so powerful in our country.*

P. Would you then demolish, at a blow, the present system of government—I mean our ostensible republican system, for I know it is not a democracy?

A. What, allow me to ask first, is your conception of a democracy?

P. *A government in which the people vote directly on every law, before they yield assent to it.*

A. *You are right. Ours is in effect an aristocracy, in which the people delegate their powers, and Legislators too often imagine for the time, all authority is theirs; and then monopolies, especial privileges and suspension, and ex post facto laws are passed, in favor of those whose immediate self-interest is involved. The people are too often hardly thought of, excepting to be overreached.*

P. But I ask again: Would you at once abandon the old doctrines of the Constitution?

(The Constitution, a "leaking vessel", and must be abandoned.—Ed.)

A. Not by any means. Not any more than if one were in a leaky vessel he should spring overboard to save himself from drowning. It is a ship put hastily together when we left the British flag, and it was then thought an experiment of very doubtful issue, and the way to reformation was left open, making treason to consist solely in raising arms against our countrymen. Reason was left free with the people to reform or build anew, and we exercise our liberty fully, only we speak, act and write as we think, under reasonable limitations.

P. You term our ostensible system of government an aristocracy. Prove it to be so, according to civilians' understanding of the term.

A. Civilians recognize only three forms of government, to wit: Democratical, in which the people act directly on every law—the Aristocratical, in which a few make laws—and the Monarchical, in which one man has absolute power to pass or suspend all laws at his own pleasure. *Our real government is then a kind of aristocracy, still unsettled, however; the contest being still between the rich and poor, and productive of hatred on one side and fear on the other.* The one party asking for severer laws, the other for no laws or system of government or restraint whatever, even for vice. The combatants are chiefly demagogues and tyrants, and mixed with the demagogues are "gentle optimists," who say, "let men alone and things will regulate themselves," and with the tyrants are many worthy men who ask only for law and order in society. *Whichever party gains the day, tyrants or demagogues are most sure to take the offices."**

P. What are your objections to the free trade system?

A. We have said before we are optimists, but you will observe, we recognize in the nature of men and things, a disposition and means of improvement by creating more and more perfect organizations. *To break down laws and constitutions, without building up a better system, is to demolish your old homestead before the new is built. We must have where to lay our heads, even if it be no better than a rookery.* Necessity must always be considered first. Men not practical, too often ask of statesmen what cannot be, consistently with the nature of

---

*Thousands of instances much like the following may be quoted, as every one can witness, and so can even worse, as late developments have proved in court. In the Manor of Pelham, a man not even fit to be a customer to a groggery, and who lost his eye in being expelled from one, and who was brought up begrimed with filth to match a negro's vote, turned the scale and elected all the officers to one of the richest towns in this state. Bad men thus turn the scale, and men of honor are too generally overlooked or laughed to scorn.

things. In their wild love of freedom, they would break down the fences on the brinks of precipices. *Free trade in absolute perfection, cannot possibly be had without some certain, precise and exact regulations, which we advocate.*

P. What for instance?

(Monetary system is base of evil.—Ed.)

A. *There must be a new mercantile system and a new kind of money or bill of exchange introduced.* The want of this is the source of one of your complaints at the commencement. You saw effects as others do, but not the cause.

P. What difficulties are there in the present system and medium of exchange?

A. The difficulties are so great that it is absolutely impossible for the great body of producers, even if men have the best possible dispositions, ever to arise to a competency under them, while they use that system and medium. *Any given amount of money, represents any amount of articles having exchangeable value, by a certain scale of prices, which is high or low, as there may be more or less money in circulation, out of the banks or mines.* Consequently, the position tacitly assumed by Dr. Adam Smith, Say, Ricardo, M'Culluch and others, that the prices in any country are an indication of the value of the articles to the people of any country, or that they indicate the advantages or disadvantages of any nation to produce or manufacture, is false. For example :—Ireland is densely populated, and often has famines, while the United States has an immense territory of soil unoccupied, and fertile, and yet we have imported beef, butter, hay and potatoes from Ireland,—starving them and glutting us—*simply because her absentees draw out their incomes and spend them abroad, and thus make prices low in Ireland; while our bankers issue paper money excessively, and create high prices and induce excessive imports on the principle of Adam Smith, Ricardo, Wayland and others,* buying cheap and selling dear, and leaving THINGS to regulate themselves. Alas; poor "things" they die, for *men are held as operative things,* and *thus are regulated, straightened for the grave, their only hope.* There is a district in Ireland remarkable for its cattle, and the houses of the peasantry have been razed to the ground to give place to brutes, which are sold dear to the contractors for the foreign armies of Great Britain. *If one ox consume as much as may sustain five men, then for every beast exported, a family is robbed of bread, in a densely populated country.*

Moreover, excessive production and excessive population so much complained of in Great Britain is, according to my view of the subject, grossly misunderstood, even by her statesmen. The appearance of these evils, which have caused the monarch to tremble on his throne, from the heavings of the mass, on which the whole superstructure is reared up, arises solely from the use of the money of the free trade theory, on the principle of prices rising and falling as money increases in proportion to money: Whenever the machinery is improved, or the people are *more than ordinarily industrious, goods increase faster than the money, to keep up their money price, and they must fall of course.* The master manufacturer cannot then continue to have more and more produced, or he would be *certain to fall to ruin himself. He therefore discharges his hands to consume their little savings, and then starve. Thus the great body of the people can never hope to arise to a competency.*

(Capitalist employer is villain.—Ed.

The evils which you have in part depicted and complained of, thus arise from the unfitness of the present system of commerce and medium of exchange, and I know too well they are absolutely appalling in the contemplation and prospect. There is no amelioration to be expected from extraordinary exertion on the poor man's part, nor can improvement in machinery assist him. *Machinery as you observe, becomes his rival. It is a nightmare, an incubus which sits upon his breast, and not in fancy but in fact, distorts his limbs, and blinds his eyes, and palsies his vital energies. His children have reason, I had almost said, to rise and curse him. He sends them through rain, sleet and snow in rags, to the heartless overseer of any factory, to inhale from morn to night its pestiferous* *vapors. It must go on or suffer its taskmaster's lash, or be cropped and shut up in a poor-house, termed as you say by the poor "bastiles," for out of them no green fields or cheerful passengers are seen.* Their windows, as you justly have complained, are blinded and like prisons. *The poor are forced to seek for parochial assistance, and then punished for their poverty when they do make an application.* If in their despair they rise in mobs, a *standing army is prepared to shoot them down.* And thus *there is no hope, and they turn to artificial stimulants, to find in temporary madness a relief from thought. Human life is shortened** and *human beings are deformed and words are like the idle wind. No mere moral or religious lessons can avail, unless men teach a better system of Political Economy and Government.*

P. This last is a grave assertion; how can you prove that vice will thus continue to prevail?

A. Before the discovery of the great improvements, in the cotton manufacturing machinery there was not a more religious or moral people in the world than those of Scotland. About the year 1800 there were only eighty commitments per annum for crime in the whole kingdom. After that discovery the weavers had to work eighteen and twenty hours of the twenty-four, to obtain a sufficiency of the poorest provisions to sustain existence, and some labored—says a report to the British House of Commons—twice a week all night long. As the improvements in machinery increased between the years 1800-20, wages fell and want increased. Wages fell from eighteen shillings sterling per week, to about four shillings, and fathers, it is said, began to teach their children to commit crime to prevent direct starvation. And crime increased to about eight hundred commitments per annum. If such has been the effect amongst some of the most moral and religious people of Europe, can morals

*The celebrated Dr. Combe has given it as his opinion that the vast proportion of the poor of Great Britain, die early of diseases superinduced by excessive labor and deficient nourishment, and yet they boast of machinery equal in power to half the number of people on the globe, and talk of excessive production of the means of comfortable living.

and religion be taught to any degree successfully, while mankind are reduced to such a state of misery? All the physical, moral and religious evils, arising from the present mercantile system and medium of exchange, cannot be condensed within the limits prescribed to this work.

P. But free trade *does not exist in England; the corn laws and the whole British system is a system of shackles on trade.* And England is obliged to deal with other nations having tariffs.

A. This does not alter the nature of the mercantile system, or the nature of money. Merchants only use a few more figures in their calculations. If they pay a duty, they charge a profit on the duty to consumers, and manufacturers compete with each other in machinery, and when allowed, obliged *little children to labor fourteen, sixteen and eighteen hours per day,* while *complaining of excessive population.* Issues and withdrawals of paper money, nullify all tariffs. When we raised our tariff highest, England curtailed her currency, and our bankers increased our circulation, and our greatest statesmen—at least those considered greatest by the vulgar, because they most agree with them—stood looking at each other—to speak figuratively—with their fingers in their mouths. From mere shame they may now desire to say nothing on the subject.

P. But does not the misery of the producing classes of Great Britain arise from excessive population?

A. No. It has been conceded by men qualified to judge, that Ireland alone, under the spade husbandry, is sufficient to supply double the population of Great Britain and Ireland. Moreover, England has machinery equal to four hundred millions of man power, *and the people are more and more in want as the great capitalists are enabled to increase their property.* There are *swamps, containing many thousands of acres as good as the Pottery Car near Doncaster,* which *was formerly a bog and now a garden yielding abundantly, but as it will not pay over two or three percent, to make investments on them,* while *manufacturing will pay perhaps from five to ten or fifteen, they are suffered still to send forth their miasms, fevers and agues; and those who might improve them, and be supported by them, are suffered to lie idle and sometimes die by the highway-side, seeking for labor,* while *it is not to the self-interest of the free trade capitalists to give employment.* In this country, though independent of all other countries, the *licentious character of the selfish free trade principle is apparent.*

P. What is your opinion of the Hamiltonian or American tariff system?

A. I have expressed it at various times in different publications, and shall briefly answer, as just hinted, that it is *self-contradictory and unworthy of a statesmen.* It *consists of two parts.* The *tariff, to encourage manufacturers by raising the prices of foreign goods so high when brought to our markets that the domestic may be preferred as cheaper;* and the banking system, to afford facilities to trade. But by the issue of paper money from the banks, prices are raised, and domestic manufactures are to a great extent neglected for the foreign articles, and no increase of the tariff, as experience has proved, can protect domestic productions, while the banks may issue paper money at their pleasure. We have fallen in debt fifteen millions of dollars annually on an average, as you have truly observed, and the nation is overwhelmed in trouble in consequence. *Its state, canal and rail road stocks are mortgaged to our ancient enemy.*

P. Why do not politicians rectify so great an oversight?

A. It is against their direct self-interest to attack the banking system in reality.

P. What do you offer them as better?

(Advocates currency manipulation and "control" and "free trade."—Ed.)

A. As an ordinary politician, the remedy we have uniformly advocated, is directly the reverse of the system of Alexander Hamilton in all its parts. On the same principle that the American system has swamped the nation in debt, a reverse of Hamilton's system will clear them of debt, and bring other nations in debt to us. In a word, we would break down the tariff and greatly reform the banking system, and regulate the nominal value of money to correspond with the real value it would have, on the withdrawal of bank paper such as we at present have.

P. Are bankers so much worse than other men, that you would have them all cut off at a blow, for the evils they have done the country?

A. Not by any means. The evils which arise from the system are not foreseen or even apprehended by many of them. They consider it the merchants' own fault for overtrading; not perceiving or *thinking that they themselves raise prices up so high, as to offer the inducement to overtrade, and that merchants are taught by our highest institutions of learning to "buy cheap and sell dear, and let good order make itself"* in the *community according to the free trade theory.* Moreover, criminations and recriminations of whole classes, are all useless. *The evils arise simply from the absence of the true principles and system of just government.* All are equally in fault, who do not seek for this the great remedy, in a perfect science of co-operation.

P. How can we seek for that of which, as yet, we nothing know?

A. You are seeking for it. To be discontented with your present lot, and to aspire to a better, is to seek for what I have now to demonstrate.

P. I pray you then proceed. What are your great designs?

A. They run side by side with Christianity; "to feed the hungry, clothe the naked, to make peace on earth, and amongst men good will."

(Christianity and God serve only to confirm "natural law."—Ed.)

P. Why do you not come out at once for christianity?

A. Because, what I have in view is an earthly government, and I desire not to elevate a hierarchy. Jesus Christ himself has taught, his kingdom was "not of this world."

P. You are not then opposed to christianity?

A. Not by any means. Christianity I hope may yields us great assistance. But a true statesman is ordained of God to read his laws in nature, and he looks with evil eye on no persuasion which the great Father of us all sees fit to tolerate. When any one would put down the "higher powers," then, and not before, should the true statesman be alive to hold his just prerogative—to give protection to all, superiority to none.

(The science of government.—Ed.)

P. How do you commence the demonstration of the science of government?

A. We consider: 1st. What are the wants of man? 2d. How are they to be supplied?

P. But the wants of man are different in various ages, times and places.

A. True. And yet our greatest wants are so similar, that, excepting in the slight differences of taste, we all agree.

Our first want is the clothing, food and shelter for the body. When these are secured,

Our second want is security for our persons and our property.

Our third want is general knowledge, refinement, amusement and glory.

We have thus the foundations of the science.

(Blueprint of "New Deal, NRA, Soviet Dictatorship.—Ed.)

FIRST ORDER.

The creating or producing arts and sciences consisting of	1. Agriculture. 2. Manufactures. 3. Commerce.

SECOND ORDER.

Preserving arts and sciences.	1. Law. 2. War. 3. Medicine.

THIRD ORDER.

Refining arts and sciences.

1. Natural History.
2. Physiology.
3. Moral Philosophy
4. Literature.
5. The Mathematics.
6. Fine Arts.

FIRST ORDER, CREATING.

	Temperate Region. 1	Warm Region. 2	Torrid Region. 3
Agriculture.	Timber, Grazing, Wheat, Flax, Hemp & Corn region.	Cotton, Rice, Orange, Fig, Vine.	Sugar, Spice, Cocoa. 4 Fishregion.

Manufactures.

1. Clothing Materials.
2. Viands.
3. Metals & Minerals.
4. Drugs, Paints, Dye Stuffs & Medicines.
5. Machinery.

Commerce.

- Bankers' House of Exchange.
- Merchants' Stores.
- Appraisers' Board.
- Sailors, Ships & Docks.

SECOND ORDER, PRESERVING.

Law.

- Court for the correction of errors.
- Police system.
- Court of Arbitration.

War.

- Army.
- Navy.

Medicine. — Central Board.

- District No. 1
- " " 2
- " " 3
- " " 4

THIRD ORDER, REFINING.

Natural History.	All the outward appearances and habits of things animate, and the changes of appearance of inanimate objects.
Physiology.	The organism of all organized Things & Beings.
Moral Philosophy.	The laws of mind. Logic. The evidences of the existence of an almighty, allwise, and perfect Creator. The motives to be presented to man: Selfish, Moral, Rational, Religious.
Literature	Modern Languages: English. French. German. Ancient Languages: Latin. Greek. Hebrew.
The Mathematics.	Arithmetic, Geometry, &c.
Fine Arts.	Painting, Poetry. Sculpture. Music. Oratory. Dancing, &c.

We here have the body of the science. The next object is to give the spirit and the moving power, and render it practical. Our object is to convert to the arts and sciences of peace, that system and principle of co-operation, now best known in war; for that is, as experience proves, the only practical system of harmonious co-operation. We have marked out the ground on which every class of mind must take its place. We have a place for every art and science, and now the tactics to be observed in each, and how to gain the land on which to operate, is all we have to show.

First, of the art and science of co-operation. This is to bring the whole to bear for our mutual advantage.

To learn the art of government correctly, men should begin to practice at the rudiments, as a soldier first learns the manual and if prompt and energetic becomes a petty officer and drills others. He then arises by degrees through every grade. It is thus that every art and science must, according to the nature of the human mind, be learnt. Some, of great quickness of perception and tact, may learn more readily than others it is true, but the system we have given is the only safe one. "An officer of a ship must creep in at the hauze hole and not through the cabin windows" according to a common maxim of sea-faring men, or they become ridiculous in action, as our politicians generally are. To hope to make a man a surgeon or physician, a moral philosopher or professor of belles-lettres, or divine, by an election of a majority, is not more absurd than to hope by the same means to make a statesman. In what condition would the arts and sciences be, if every year or two a new election and a general change should be effected, by electing hatters to be shoe makers; shoe makers, tailors; tailors, lawyers; lawyers, sailors; sailors, divines; divines, soldiers; soldiers, merchants, and thus on?

P. We should retrograde to barbarism!

A. Yes. We could depend on nothing being done correctly.

P. But as your system has not been in operation, how can it commence?

Where will you find practically instructed officers?

A. The greatest difficulty lies indeed in the first steps. But by dividing and subdividing, and simplifying all their duties, the risk of failure is so lessened that, as armies have been heretofore well officered and prepared for active service by a previous exercise, by like means and by degrees, may we also accomplish our object. *I refer you to the diagrams, by which the bearings and dependencies of all the parts, may be at a glance perceived. On this, the lines of accountability are shown converging to a point from each inferior to a superior officer, and the superior being in like manner accountable with others to a higher. We thus go on, until one is enabled to perceive at a glance where anything is wrong in government, and apply the remedy, by holding the officer having charge of the department accountable at once.*

P. To whom should the officers be accountable, should the superior not perceive?

A. *To the people who may suffer.*

P. Who will try the question?

A. *The Court for the Correction of Errors.*

P. How will that Court be formed?

A. The Grand Marshall will retire at the termination of two, three or four years, from the time of his accession to the chief command, and after that he will be a judge, immovable, unless for imbecility, insanity or immorality.

P. Who shall decide this point?

A. The people may accuse him to his peers, and they shall try him when the number of his accusers shall amount to twenty-four good and respectable citizens.

P. What security have you that they will impartially do justice?

A. Regard for the honor of their body, natural consciousness, and the desire to be relieved of all annoyance, and sustain a system in which they have gained their honors.

P. What is the general duty of officers?

A. To see that those in the next rank below them do their duty, while they in the mean time do their own special duty.

P. What are the especial duties of each class of officers?

A. They are as numerous and as various as the wants of man. There will be a class for the supply of every reasonable want, and an officer accountable for the supply.

P. Will the men be strictly accountable to the officers, and be forced to labor for a certain time daily, willing or unwilling, as soldiers are obliged to drill?

A. There will be no constraint other than Providence has now established. *Those who labor most will gain the most, while those who labor less will have the less.* The officer has only to calculate correctly on the dispositions of his men. He is to learn how much a certain number of industrious and indolent men will on an average produce. A superior officer will supply men, fitted by their natural organization to excel in every branch of art and science, on the requisition of any proper officer.

P. Whose duty will it be to make appointments to each class?

(Grand Marshal—the "Fuhrer."—Ed.)

A. The Grand Marshal's.

P. Who will be accountable that the men appointed are the best qualified?

A. A Court of Physiologists, Moral Philosophers, and Farmers and Mechanics, to be chosen by the Grand Marshal and accountable to him.

P. Would you constrain a citizen to submit to their decisions in the selection of a calling?

A. No. If any one of good character insisted, he might try until he found the occupation most congenial to his tastes and feelings.

P. Would not this create confusion?

A. Not at all. Few are *desirous of undergoing all the awkwardnesses of new occupations, when once their "hands are in." Men also pride themselves on their consistency and steadiness of purpose, for nothing marks a strong mind so truly, as steadiness of purpose in any great design.*

P. Will it not have a bad effect upon the constitution, to confine men, or suffer them to confine themselves to certain occupations?

A. *Men need not labor so long under a proper system of division of labors, to produce subsistence, as at present; for now, not only do accumulators reap the fruits of industry, but lonely labors are not so productive as associated labors, by a vast amount.* Athletic sports and exercise of military arms, should relieve the toil-worn manufacturer and producer—*music, dancing and games of skill and judgment, all are proper in their times and places to prevent diseases of the body and the mind.* But each man should learn some part of some useful *trade or science perfectly, to make him independent.* Each *should have his proper place, where he might be dependent on to some extent, and know that he was useful to society.*

(A "managed economy"—Ed.)

P. What is the duty of the Marshal of the Creating or Producing order?

A. It is to estimate the amount of produce and manufactures necessary to produce a sufficiency in each department below him. When in operation, he shall report excesses and deficiencies to the Grand Marshal.

P. How shall he discover such excesses and deficiencies?

A. The various merchants will report to him the demand and supplies in every line of business, as will be seen hereafter.

P. Under this order are agriculture, manufactures and commerce, as I perceive. What then is the duty of the Marshal of Agriculture?

A. He should have under him four regions, or if not, foreign commerce must make good the deficiency.

P. What four regions?

A. The temperate, the warm, the hot region and the water region.

P. Why divide them thus?

A. Because the products of these different regions require different systems of cultivation, and are properly subject to different minds.

P. Are not the different products of each region also various?

A. They are, and there is a natural succession of crops suited to each kind of soil. As for instance, the alternation of the white and green crops, which retains the soil's productiveness.

P. What do you mean by white and green crops?

A. It is a technicality used by scientific agriculturalists to indicate grain and roots, by which the necessity for fallows is avoided, and the land, by the system indicated, continues to increase in fer-

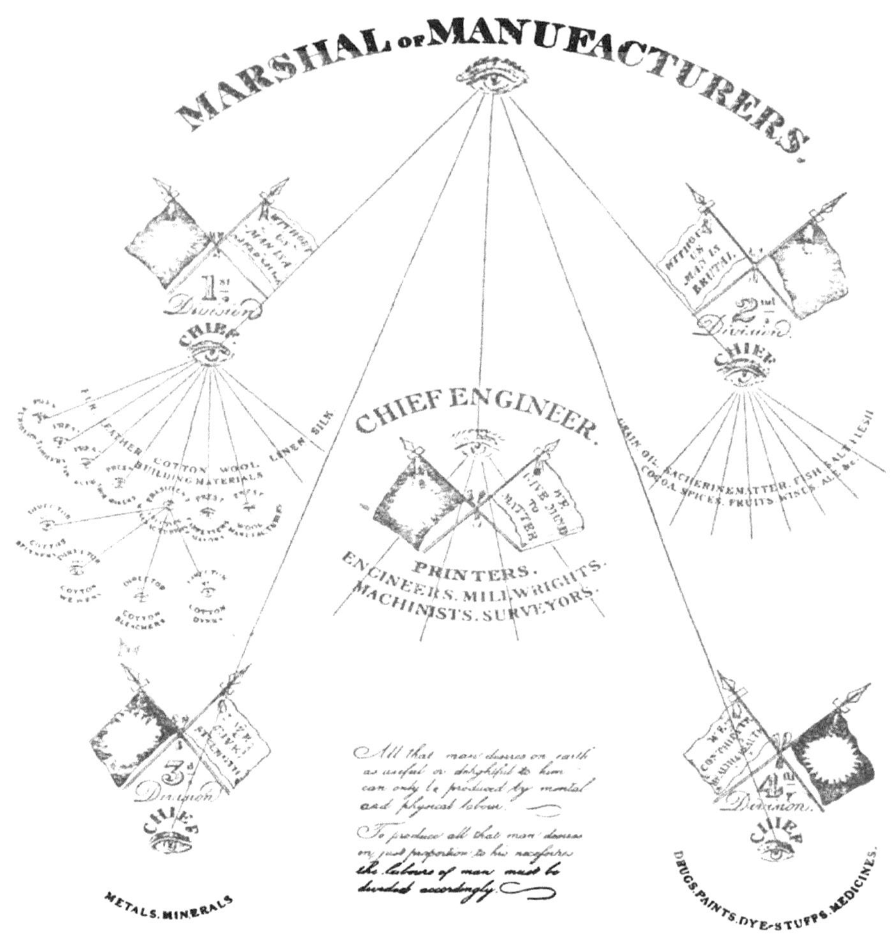

BLUEPRINT OF THE "NEW DEAL" NRA

N(ATIONAL) R(ECOVERY) A(DMINISTRATION)

Drawn up by Clinton Roosevelt in 1841, as the basis of a Communist dictatorship, and put in force by his cousin Franklin Delano Roosevelt ninety-two years later.

tility. The white consists of grain, the green of turnips, beets, carrots and potatoes, &c. For the routine of crops, each section of each region must have its proper officer accountable to his superior.

P. Should every section be divided into individual possessions, as at present?

A. *No.* Men *should work in large companies together, and the time of labor of each individual should be kept, if he could hold his place in the rank or do a fair day's work.*

P. What if not of average strength?

A. He must choose some other occupation or be content to work with boys, and take a part of a day's work for the time necessary to constitute a day of labor.

P. What if any man should have the strength and skill to do the work of two?

A. He *should receive certificates accordingly?*

P. Will it not be difficult to estimate a fair day's work?

A. *Not by any means. In almost every kind of work, it is already well established.*

P. What is to be done with the produce of the soil.

A. *It is to be lodged in the graineries and stores of the community.*

P. How then can the producers receive the fruits of ther own labors?

A. This question will be answered under the commercial system and medium of exchange.

P. There are some occupations of husbandmen which are manufacturing, such as wine-pressing, cider and sugar making, cotton ginning, &c. Would you separate these from the callings of the husbandmen?

A. *Where labors can be advantageously divided, the division should take place, but not otherwise.*

P. What other duties should devolve upon the *marshal of husbandmen?*

A. He should observe the seasons, and if any drought, excessive frost, or cut worms, should destroy a crop, he shall give out notice that a substitute be sown or planted. As for instance, should the winter grain be frozen out, he should recommend spring wheat, buckwheat and potatoes, and greater crops of Indian corn. *He should publish also the best systems of husbandry, or at least observe that such be published.*

P. What are the duties of the *Marshal of Manufacturers?*

A. He shall divide men into five general classes, according to the printed diagram.

1st. The manufacturers of all the means of defence against the weather.

2d. All kinds of viands.

3d. Metals and minerals.

4th. Chemicals.

5th. Machinery.

All these have on the printed diagrams, banners, with a glory on one side and an appropriate motto on the reverse, showing the advantage each class is to all others: and by the way, we would remark, this should be universally adopted, to give a just direction to man's love of glory.

By a reference to the chart, and what has been before observed, the duties of the officers under this department will all be obvious.

P. What will be the duty of the Marshal of the Commercial Region?

A. Under him, in the first diagram, will be observed a house of appraisers, stores and docks, and house of exchange, &c.

The evils of the present mercantile system and medium of exchange, or money of commerce, should now be recalled to mind. This is to rectify those innumerable and crying evils. As follows:

Wherever any articles are produced or finished, they are taken by the owners of the house of appraisers, and there men in every branch of art may find persons to value what may be presented.

The valuation is direct, and not through the medium of specie or the shadow of specie, paper based on specie, lands or other property.

P. What do you mean by *direct valuations?*

A. At present, all money values are indirect estimates of the time of labor accumulated on any article or property. Indirect, because the precious metals are valued by the time of labor it requires to produce any certain amount, and then all other property is valued through that medium.

But in this system, the valuation takes place immediately, without the intervention of the precious metals. The valuation is by the time of labor it has generally cost to produce the like to what it is to be valued.

When this valuation is obtained, the article is taken to the proper store or arcade, and there deposited with the price marked on it, and the maker's names.

The producer or manufacturer next goes to the house of exchange, taking with him the certificate of deposit and also of appraisement. He then in return receives bills of exchange, engraved like a bank bill of the same form, and worded as follows:

"On demand, the Eclectic Association promises to deliver to the bearer the produce of one day's labor." To be signed and countersigned.

If the amount be larger or smaller, the common divisions of time determine the required amount, as hours, weeks, months and years.

By this simple process there can be no stagnations of trade, or appearance of excessive production or population, or usury, or bankruptcy, or want of any kind, in any man disposed to labor. All may be absolutely certain of a competency, and none need suffer as at present, when banks refuse to discount.

No distortions of the body from excessive fatigue, nor early death from long continued deficiencies of nourishment. No desperation from want, nor crime, nor blasphemy of the Deity, because those who earn all secure nothing, while those who do nothing valuable to society accumulate the fruits of industry of all others.

P. How can you prevent excessive issues?

A. This is a most important consideration, and the community should guard this bank of currency with the most jealous care, for the right to coin and issue money is one of the highest prerogatives of sovereignty. The people must always hold the reins themselves. The purse in one hand, and the sword in the other, is the preservative against all great danger from the highest officers.

The bank books, therefore, should be offered at a certain hour daily to the people, that every entry of every clerk might be examined and if any credit should be given to any unknown man, the certificates of deposits may be called for, and these, if found, will at one direct to the store or arcade where his productions have been lodged. Should no such articles be found, a forgery or fraudulent issue will be self-evident, and the proper officer will have to answer for it. Should the amount be large, and prove connivance or a want of caution, the officer will be dismissed with disgrace.

Various officers being thus personally liable for every false issue, and degraded and disgraced at once for every wrong a degree of security will be arrived at equal to that which now obtains in the Post Office, where each clerk and officers holds a check upon those who deliver and those who receive valuable letters. The degree of safety and certainty is therefore admirable under that system.

Abstracts from the books shall be published daily by the Marshal of the Creating Order, and every one shall be shown when he desires, that the books do correspond with such publications.

P. What shall be the duty of the merchants?

A. To receive and give certificates of deposit for all property left with them for sale. To take an account of all demands for goods or buildings, and inform the marshals of the classes of producers having in charge the supply of the deficient articles, on which he as before remarked applies for men to the Grand Marshal.

P. What shall be done when there is an overplus of any articles?

A. *It shall be the duty of the merchants to inform the Marshal of the Commercial Department, who shall examine and order an export, and send supercargoes to obtain supplies of whatever products the region of country will not produce abundantly. Specie may thus be introduced as an article of commerce.*

P. What shall be the duty of the Port Admiral?

A. To report on the state of the ships and docks,

and take proper care of the marine department in commerce.

P. Who will have charge of other means of transportation, such as locomotive engines, &c.?

A. The chief engineer and his department.

P. How can house carpenters and joiners, masons, &c., lodge any of their works in the stores, and as they cannot, how can they be remunerated?

A. Persons requiring houses, lodge the specification and plan in the builder's stores, and an estimate is made of the time of labor necessary to finish every part, just as master builders now estimate when they make contracts. At the finishing of every part, the appraisers of buildings will be called, and certificates of the amount of labor done will be left in the builders' department, and a certificate of such deposit will be given, and with this in hand the mechanic may go to the house of exchange, and draw bills as any other mechanic might do, were the goods, instead of what answers for the deed of the house, deposited.

P. *How will a citizen be paid for any new invention in the arts or sciences?*

A. An estimate of the amount of labor it is calculated to save, will first be made by the appraisers. The number who will be thrown out of employment for a time must be taken into account, and then a yearly payment of a certain proportion of the neat profit shall be considered the inventor's right for life, or until some superior invention shall supercede it.

P. Will not such great profits in the hands of inventors tend to create an aristocracy of wealth?

A. It is not in the nature of inventors to hoard. The fascination of the inventive power leads to great sacrifices in experiments, and not more than one invention in twelve succeeds and becomes practically useful. Moreover, the possession of wealth will give no citizen an advantage in law, or government, or arms. It can only create greater elegance, which can not do real injury to any individual.

P. How can the share of inventors be collected?

A. In the same manner and at the same time that commissions of merchants and means of paying officers, and interest on the debt for lands, and other liabilities which at first may have to be provided for.

P. How will all this be done?

A. A discount will be made from the appraisement and certificates, and bills will be given accordingly.

P. What amount of discount will be made?

A. That will depend upon the liabilities of the association for lands and outfit.

P. Do you advocate a national or state debt?

A. We must submit to circumstances. If we cannot remove without contracting a debt which it will require some extra labor to pay, it is better to endure the extra work, than toil without hope of final competency.

P. Have not the exchange bills been tried by Robert Owen, and did they not fail in the experiment

A. Yes, in part; in 1833 in London.

P. If they failed then, why will they succeed under your system?

A. Because we have a mercantile system in connexion, which he had not. It has been herein explained. It is to keep a full supply of every article constantly, and not allow any to exhaust the stores of any one article. The wants of man being regular, any attempt by strangers to run the stores short of any article should be at once resisted by the merchants. The surplus might be sold in any quantity at any time, but a sufficiency for the regular demands of the association must always be preserved in store. The means of doing this have been already explained.

P. The next order is the preserving, and I find under it Law, War and Medicine. What law do you adopt?

A. The simplest possible.

P. Which is that?

A. That written on our hearts by the finger of God Almighty, and applicable at all times and places. It consists of only one sentence, to wit: whatsoever ye would not that another should do by you, that do you not by others, on pain of expulsion or confinement until reformed.

P. How will you bring this universal law to bear upon society practically?

A. *I take it for granted, that if impartial men generally, cannot, on a plain statement of a case, distinguish right from wrong, no books can teach it them, because wanting perception, they cannot distinguish between wise and unwise books of laws.*

Moreover, the attempt to specify every act which should not be committed, is to attempt an absolute impossibility; because there are so many acts which are improper that the attempt to specify them all only leaves every variety of wrong open to the artful, and thus gives a tacit consent to wrong.

*The absurdities of the Anglo-Roman laws, which prevail in our country, are too numerous to be mentioned here.**

P. In case of any difficulty between citizens, what shall be the course to be pursued by the injured party?

A. *The complaint shall be laid before the Marshal of the Law, and he shall cause an officer to issue summons to a jury, to be drawn by ballot, one for each of thirteen different occupations. A jury of thirteen shall thus be called, and the majority shall decide the case on the principles of equity,* and *cause full restitution to be made for any act of fraud or force;* and *if violence should have been committed, the criminal should be considered as a man subject to temporary madness, and confined in an hospital until the temperament and will, be changed by proper regimen and instruction.*

P. What! would you treat moral diseases medically, under your system?

A. Certainly. Depletion is the proper remedy for men subject to outrageous passions. Depletion will tame tigers and lions. High feeding insult and fullness of blood only tend to make the matter worse. Vegetable diet and sufficient instruction and labor is the remedy for an outrageous disposition, if the organism be not defective.

P. Would you not hang a murderer?

A. No. We should only confine him as we would

---

*The author has a lecture written on this subject, which he may publish hereafter.

a ravenous wild beast. It *is wrong to disgrace their relatives, and it is beneath the dignity of society to take revenge on any individual.*

P. Is not that principle of Jewish law a good one, by which an eye is demanded for an eye, and a tooth for a tooth?

A. It is in general, since we can only sympathize with such as we have wronged, by suffering as they have suffered, and sympathy is one of the greatest incentives to virtue. *But a dead man cannot sympathize and it tends to brutalize the mind to witness brutal punishments.*

P. How would you render the awards of juries practical?

A. By the police system.

P. How should that system be arranged?

A. Just as the militia system is arranged at present. All of an active age and powers should be enrolled, and the people should take their turns on guard in order to preserve society unharmed.

P. Should they not be paid for detecting and capturing freebooters?

A. No. It leads to the "stool-pigeon" system, by which the officers themselves are led to prey upon society. It must never be made to the interest of any officer to do anything in opposition to the general good.

P. What pay should they then receive?

A. The same as if at any other occupation which they may have left. They should be rewarded for their tact and courage by the thanks and praises of their fellow citizens.

(Law frowned upon.—Ed.)

P. Would you have no forms of law, nor deeds or instruments of writing?

A. They might be recommended by the marshal of the law department, but should not be arbitrary. He *might also recommend a simple code of laws, but it should not be absolute with any jury.* The *natural sense of right and wrong should always be left free.*

P. Would you have no pleaders or lawyers?

A. I would have orators, and have them follow nature, but *none should have an entree to the courts, to the exclusion, as now, of any class or individual.*

P. If there were no written laws, what could they do?

A. Appeal to conscience, after plainly stating all the circumstances and proving them, as some men are not possessed of fluency, to do so in their own behalf.

P. Would you allow any person to give evidence in his own case?

A. Certainly. I would never rule evidence out of court, however slight or unworthy of belief it might appear. *Nor should we believe any absolutely, for all may be mistaken even when with the best intentions, since our passions lead our minds astray, and "what ardently we wish we soon believe."*

P. The second Genus of the Preserving or Protecting order is the War department, the first species of which is the army, second the navy. What say you on this head?

A. In the science and art of war, we recognize the nearest approach to perfection under existing things. Time may suggest improvements in arms and tactics but the true principle of co-operation exists in the navy as well as army.

P. Would you have a class of citizens bred to arms for the protection of the state?

(Universal miltary training—Ed.)

A. No: all should be bred to arms. *It should constitute a part of the education of every youth. To give one class a knowledge of the practice of arms and not others, is to raise up a class of tyrants to oppress their fellow-citizens. Liberty is safe only when the sword, the press and legislative power, are preserved by the people in their own hands, and never delegated to others.*

By a reference to the first diagram, it will be seen that the army falls into its place, without any alteration of its arrangements.

P. At what age should citizens be subject to military duty.

A. Between the ages of eighteen and forty-five, and in cases of invasion at any age over eighteen, when able to do duty.

P. How would you man the navy?

A. *By volunteers from the mercantile shipping, and by naval schools instructing boys.*

(State medicine an essential for scheme. —Ed.)

P. The third Genus under the Preserving order is medicine. How is this department to be conducted differently from the present mode?

A. It must be made to the immediate self-interest of physicians to prevent diseases, and not to have sickness, as at present.

P. How is this possible?

A. By the following arrangement. Let the community or nation be divided into districts, and let each district be subdivided into as many classes, as there may be advocates for the different *principles of medical jurisprudence, and let each advocate arrange himself under that system which he may prefer, and those who have no preference will be drawn for by lot, until each physician have as many as he can attend to.*

It will be his duty then to prevent them from becoming ill, by proper instruction and advice, and detecting premonitory symptoms.

His pay will be by the head, and be so much the higher as there may be fewer ill under his care, and it shall stop for all who may fall ill, until they recover. The physicians shall be salaried officers.

P. Will it not be unfair to cause all to contribute to physicians' salaries?

A. *Not by any means. Diseases are contagious in many cases, and the miasm arising from squalid wretchedness sends forth pestilence to the inmate of the palace. Hereditary diseases also are transmitted by inter-marriages. For these and other reasons, bodily disease should be guarded against by the community, as much as moral diseases which result in crimes against the people.*

P. What is to prevent physicians from neglecting incurable persons.

A. A point of honor and conscience, and a coroner's inquest to be held in all cases, as when a naval officer loses a ship in battle.

P. What if neglect or mal-practice be discovered.

A. He shall be degraded, suspended, or fined or

imprisoned, according to the sentence of a court, to be summoned by the command of the marshal of the preserving order for the trial of such cases.

P. What other duties shall devolve on the medical fraternity?

A. The care and cure of moral diseases in criminals.

P. What is the cause of crimes against society?

A. *Want of sympathy,* or *extreme want, or fullness of blood or bile, exasperating the passions; also whatever in diet tends to stimulate and elevate the animal above the intellectual and moral nature of man.*

P. Are crimes then the result of want of sympathy and bad or improper diet, and subject to the skill of the physician?

A. When the organization of the individual is not radically bad, we have only to remove the cause of moral or physical diseases, and the effects will cease. As the body is convulsed by deleterious influences in the system, so is the mind which is wounded by the body politic the enemy of that body, and likely to produce disorders.

P. What is the remedy for want of sympathy, the immediate cause of crime against society?

A. Solitary confinement, and the occasional visits of a humane and mild individual, of strong sympathies, not given to canting, but with much common sense to see that he himself under like temptations might have fallen.

P. Can men of good natural feeling ever be criminals?

(Law and the State pervert men.—Ed.)

A. Certainly. As society is now organized, injustice often drives the conscientious man to do what he would not, because the law yields him neither justice, nor protection. Even a strong indignation against wrong drives him to revenge. Such men should be soothed, and not exasperated more, as they are at present. By teaching them the nature of their minds, and how to regulate their passions by reducing their diet, or if in extreme want, placing them in the way to honest competency, radical cures can in such men be effected.

P. Will not the sanitary department have a double and most onerous duty to perform for small remuneration? Who, in such a case, would study or take a physician's office?

A. It will be one of the most responsible in the system, and therefore should be held amongst the most honorable: as to remuneration, the pay may be high enough for the healthy to compensate for the carelessness of the ill and unhealthy.

If it should be proved that a physician had given fair warning of disease from a certain course of life, and the patient persisted, the physician should not lose his just remuneration, were the jury of physicians to confirm the opinion of the proper physician, whose advice had been contemned.

P. Do you apprehend much evil in society from the want of such a sanatary system as this above proposed?

A. According to human nature and the nature of things, the evils of improper medical practice must now be incalculable; because in general, what produces momentary good, such as mercury, narcotics, essential oils and other stimulants and irritants, preys at last upon the constitution and it is to the direct self-interest of physicians to be plausible and popular, rather than to cure radically, and the fault of the practitioner cannot be laid to his charge.

At present, the community have no test of the merit of different systems of medicine, or of different physicians; but under this political science the average age at which men under the various systems of medicine might die, would afford the only certain test to laymen of their various merits or demerits.

(Education to be "refining" by propaganda and "brain-washing"—Ed.)

P. The next great order is termed the Refining. Why so?

A. Because its object is to give the highest finish to the human mind.

P. What is the course of study under this department.

A. It alternates with occupation in the useful

arts and means of defence, under the two preceding orders.

P. What is the course under this order especially?

("Progressive" Education must amuse and permit pupils to do as they wish.—Ed.)

A. Throughout the whole system the study is to follow nature, and the same principle is here pursued.

The first care then is to store the youthful mind with a knowledge of all the things in nature, rather than letters and mere words, which convey no ideas until the things they represent have first been seen or understood.

The school room of even the youngest should therefore be a perfect lyceum of natural history, containing specimens of every object in nature having a name.

The names of all these things should first be taught. This is the alphabet, or part of it.

The second course of lectures will show the organization of all organized things and beings. As a child, after being amused with any curious toy, breaks it up to see how it operates, or cuts open a pair of bellows to look for the wind, from a laudable desire to know from whence it comes, curiosity thus shows the appetite for knoweldge, and it should be gratified by degrees as the capacity enlarges.

It should never be disgusted or gorged by improper nourishment, but on the contrary be made the source of pleasures of the highest character.

The next course in order, after natural history and physiology, is moral philosophy. Because, after learning the outward appearances of things and their organisms, we desire to learn the laws of the spirits which animate and move them to act. This is the highest of all the genera of the great science. It is connected with physiology by phrenology.

Whether all of the powers and passions of the human mind can be discovered or not—and it is not pretended by the writer they can be in every case—still on the degree of perfection of the body and nervous system generally, including the brain, depends the sanity or insanity of the individual or the capacity for higher or lower mental excellence; and moral disposition also depends first upon the conditions above named, and secondly on the circumstances which incite the brain generally, or any particular organs, to act.

Supposing the system of society we now are advocating to be correct, and calculated to bring all under favorable circumstances, after teaching phrenology from the crania of well known individuals, the next science to be taught are logic and the mathematics.

Thirdly. The evidences of the existence of an almighty, allwise and infinitely good Creator. The object of this is, to prevent superstitions and give men faith to pursue great designs, which require time and energy and genius for their accomplishment.

Fourthly. The next is the law of motives we have in the present work advocated, from which we inferred that no system of government, which looks not to this law, could be sustained. So great is its importance.

Fifthly. The proper motives to be presented to man to lead him to happiness.

P. What place do you give to literature and the fine arts?

A. We consider them as elegant amusements, and therefore of a virtuous tendency.

P. When should youth begin to acquire literary knowledge?

A. When they desire to remember the names of subjects of natural history.

P. When should youth begin to learn the various refining arts?

A. As soon as they acquire the taste and ask for the instruction, professors should be ready, and the community should pay the salary, inasmuch as every intellectual amusement and elegant entertainment is a preserative from idleness, which leads to crime; and the cost of prevention is better than curing a disease, moral or physical.

P. Allow me now to ask you various questions, which were not in place under any certain order.

For instance:

1st. *Where can you find lands suitable, and by what tenure would you hold them, and who is there to purchase them, when it is to the immediate self-interest of men of property to go on accumulating vast estates, and to the immediate self-interest of the poor to live from hand to mouth?*

A. As to lands, we can find in the west some most desirable tract on which to commence, and in a short time, go to and from this city, by the line of rail-roads. We are certain we may take nearly all of the advantages of an old settlement into a new country, and thus secure the good of both at once, if we only look for proper men of industry, skill and virtuous habits. In consequence of the failure of their banking systems, land of the highest quality is selling for far less than the rent of lands in our older settlements. We have heard of good cleared lands at seventy-five cents per acre.

You ask next, who is there to purchase them?

There are several small associations now in progress, and each has chosen two, to represent them in a central board. This board is to make enquiries and report when the necessary preliminaries shall have all been settled. But other small associations must be raised, and each twenty-five individuals shall be entitled to send two delegates to the central board.

As to the immediate self-interest of men of capital, if possessed of large tracts superior to the lands of Government, they will be most happy to make sale to us, inasmuch as we must at once commence a town upon the lands, and raise mills and make improvements to increase its value very greatly. This gives the best of all securities, even if we should desire to raise capital on mortgage for the present, to assist such as might not be able to assist themselves. *We hold that the greatest wealth consists in genius and industry, and the system of division of labors by which that skill and industry may best be brought to bear.* Should we be obliged to raise a stock at first, on the same principle as the national debt of any government is raised, how could it be otherwise than most secure to any lender, were all equally to enter into bonds to pay the interest on the loan. If we take no bad members into our society, and exclude distilleries and drunkards, and speculators, and other jockies without any useful means of living, we must succeed even with ordinary means; but with a system of industry as perfect as the operations of an army, in which each officer and man knows precisely what to do, and that each citizen is helping all others, while he labors in the system; security as perfect as human institutions will admit of will be given.

As to the immediate self-interest of the poor to live from hand to mouth, and not look after means of rising to a competency, their immediate self-interest will be changed when all is prepared. Those who are willing to go forward first, must be in rather better circumstances than succeeding settlers need be. It will be necessary to undergo privations at the outset; but what young man need care, if for a while he should be forced to lead a hunter's life and raise a camp of bark to live in, if in age he may look round upon a farm or factory, and boast that he had courage to step forward when few others had as much? And who that has real manly courage would not much prefer to struggle with the forest than with men, where each must snatch from others' mouths the bread, begrudged to all contending parties by hard-hearted landlords whose only calculation is the capacity of tenants to bear heavier rents?

(Private ownership of property replaced by "Soviet" ownership.—Ed.)

P. By what tenure would you hold the soil?

A. *The system should rule, and the system should look chiefly to the general good.* The soil should be owned as the capital of a stock company is owned, but no one shall vote upon his stock. And the officers shall have the right to pay off the debt at any time, but the holders of the stock shall not have the right to demand payment while the interest continues to be paid. In *a word it should be taken and paid on the same principle that the national debt of England is raised and payable.*

P. Should not every man have a certain amount of land as his own exclusive property?

A. Any individual might have a site for a house and garden, and even a farm, where it might be difficult to bring large numbers to labor together, as in some mountainous regions; but where large numbers might congregate, they should labor together under leaders in the fields, and in factories under foremen and officers, precisely as soldiers in an army do.

P. Why so much precision?

A. Because, the more perfect the discipline, the more certain the results from great bodies of men; and the more loose and slovenly the discipline, the less confidence will all practical men have in the end to be attained.

P. Many may not bear so much command from petty officers as soldiers do.

A. The respect will not be paid to the officers, but to the system. An officer without his badge of office, shall be laughed at even by boys, when he presumes to give command. And when out of the field or workshop, his authority shall cease entirely. But the higher officers who must be on duty constantly, must always be respected, although they can give no orders to the people. Each class must receive its orders only through its proper officers—those directly over them.

P. Why make this arrangement?

A. That the people may not feel constraint from any source, or at any time when discipline may not be necessary.

P. Will you not take all power from the people's hands by this arrangement?

("Rule of the proletariat"—Ed.)

A. The people will have the whole power of the purse, and sword, and legislature, all the time in their own hands literally. They will all be soldiers, and the exchange account will be subject to their constant supervision, and as jurors they may nullify the code which the marshal of the law department may present to them, and overrule and fix the damages and decide the guilt or innocence of prisoners, and *as members of the national guard, they will have no petty tyrants as officers of the police.* They will themselves take this responsibility successively.

The most perfect liberty, responsibility and scientific precision, even in the smallest particulars of government, will be the point at which to aim, and the result must be a body having many thousand, and eventually it is ardently to be desired, millions of minds, actuated by one motive and one will—one soul, and that spirit of peace and good will to all.

(Unionization for discipline not for comfort. —Ed.)

The power of the union, discipline and division of labor, and such principles of government, will give such advantages to this system, that while it will be the easiest thing possible to live under it, it will be as impossible to resist it as for an undisciplined mob or horde of barbarians to resist a regular army of soldiers. We have only to say in conclusion, we hope those who approve, may not want the moral courage to support the system at least, if not all the principles by which the author has endeavored to establish it. We may arrive at the same resting place by various roads. Philosophy and christianity need not be at variance when the end of each is to "feed the hungry and clothe the naked," and create an universal bond of sympathy. *The man who will not use his influence in supoprt of any well-digested system, to relieve the miseries of men, cannot be an advocate of any creed of true good will to man—he is no christian—for christianity consists not in making mere professions of faith,* and *saying Lord, Lord! says the great founder himself, but in doing the will of God, and what that will is may be known by the terms of final approval and condemnation, for says he, "I was an hungered and ye gave me meat, thirsty and ye gave me drink, naked and ye clothed me, sick and in prison, and ye ministered unto me; and inasmuch as ye did it to one of the least of these my brethren, ye did it unto me." And when they asked him who his brethkren were, he referred to the speechless man who had fallen amongst thieves, and could not help himself from the way side.* The *reviled Samaritan who assisted the distressed, was held up as an example to the faith-boasting Pharisee.*

(Religions pervert human minds and must conform or be abolished—Ed.)

There is much in the view which many take of christianity, which has not convinced the understanding, and consequently has not gained the assent, of the author of this system. *He belongs to no sect, and has not as yet formed his religious creed.* But he desires especially the cooperation of conscientious christians, and particularly the ministry of every sect, who teach not open blasphemy, and weeping and wailing in the place of laudable exertion in behalf of the distressed. There are men who throw stones when to them the poor do cry for bread, and who, when asked for fish or meat, *do give a serpent in some dogma, and poison the existence they should strive to render happy.* With such do we desire no communion. *Next to the government of money, a hierarchy most enslaves the mind, and tramples in the dust the noblest principles of our nature.* Away with them. We ask no man to join us, if he be not willing to stand upon the ground with other men, and seek no aid from institutions in which all may not equally partake according to the perfection of his nature on the eternal principles of equal rights, natural laws and justice.

THE END.

BIBLIOGRAPHY

Brown, Wm., An Oration 1799

Cardoso, Joaquin, El Communismo y la conspiracion contra el orden cristiano

Clymer, Reuben Swinburne, The Sacred College of Ancient Mysteries

Dwight, Timothy, The Duty of Americans in the Present Crisis

Gachot, Edward, L'Allemagne contre Napoleon; les Illumines

Jacoby, Daniel, Dar Stifter des Illuminatenorden

Laroche du Maine (J.P.L. de) Marquis de Luchots, Essai sur la Secte des Illumines

Lathrop, Joseph, A sermon on the dangers of the times

Magre, Maurice, Magicians, Seers & Mystics

Morse, Jedediah, A. sermon delivered May 9, 1798. A Warning Against the Illuminati and Their Masonic Affiliations
A sermon delivered on Thanksgiving Day, 1798

Nicolai, Cristoph Friederich, Open explanation of his membership in Order of Illuminati

Parish, Elijah, An oration delivered at Byfield, July 4, 1799

Payson, Seth, Proofs of the real existence and dangerous tendency of Illuminism

Ribani, Ameen F., The Descent of Bolshevism

Robison, J., Proofs of a conspiracy against all religious and governments of Europe carried on in secret meetings of Freemasons, Illuminati and reading societies.

Smith, John Cotton, An oration delivered at Sharon, July 4, 1798

Tappan, David, A discourse in the Chapel at Harvard College, June 19, 1798, to graduating class on the influence of the Illuminati on religion and the French Revolution.

Weishaupt, Adam, Die neuesten Arbeiten des Spartacus u. Philo in den Illuminaten-Orden, 1794
Das verbesserten System der Illuminaten mit allen Einrichtungen u. Graden, 1787
Apologie der Illuminaten

Wood, John, A full exposition of the Clintonian faction of the Society of Columbian Illuminati—with an account of the writer

Zwackh, Franz Xaverum, Einige Originalschriften

Ogden, John Cosens, A View of New England Illuminati—who are indefatigably engaged in destroying religion and the government of the United States undr a feigned regard for their safety. 1799

Webster, Nesta H., World Revolution — A Plot Against Civilization

Stauffer, Vernon, New England and the Bavarian Illuminati

Geeitner, A., Der Ingolstadter Universitatsprofessor Adam Weishaupt und seine Geheimbund der Illuminaten.

Schulz, Hans, Adam Weishaupt

Winrod, Gerald Burton, Adam Weishaupt, A Human Devil.

Cigrand, B. J., Story of the Great Seal of the U.S.

Totten, Chas. A. L., The Seal of History — Our Inheritance, the Great Seal of Manassch

Moses, Ernest C., Our U.S. Some Facts About the Nation's Seal
Morey, Grace Kincaid, Mystic Americanism
State Department, History of the Seal of the U.S.
The Seal of the U.S.
De Vos, Cornelius, The Unfinished Work of the U.S. of America—Its Origin, Mission & Destiny as Revealed in its Unused Seal & the Holy Scriptuures.
Rockefeller Foundation, Annual Reports.
Council on Foreign Relations, (Annual) Report of Director
Whittelsey, Charles Barney, Roosevelt Genealogy
Josephson, Emanuel M., The Strange Death Of Franklin D. Roosevelt
Rockefeller "Internationalist," The Man Who Misrules The World.

INDEX

INDEX (continued)

INDEX (continued)